THE
EXCELLENCE
HABIT

HOW SMALL CHANGES IN OUR MINDSET CAN MAKE A BIG DIFFERENCE IN OUR LIVES

VLAD ZACHARY

CENTRAL STREET PUBLICATIONS

THE EXCELLENCE HABIT

HOW SMALL CHANGES IN OUR MINDSET CAN MAKE A BIG DIFFERENCE IN OUR LIVES

FOR ALL WHO FEEL STUCK

For information about special discounts for bulk purchases, please visit http://vladzachary.com/

ISBN-13: 978- 0692674796

ISBN-10: 1519256612

Library of Congress Control Number: 2015919961

PRINTED IN THE UNITED STATES OF AMERICA

To Martin and Amelia

And to my wife, Tatyana

Thank you

"We are what we repeatedly do. Excellence, then, is not an act, but a habit."

— Aristotle
As paraphrased by Will Durant in his book *The Story of Philosophy: The Lives and Opinions of the World's Greatest Philosophers*

"It is not the mountain we conquer, but ourselves."

— Edmund Hillary,
First man on Everest

Table of Contents

EXCELLENCEOLOGY

Most of us have two lives. The first one is the life we actually live; the second is the imagined life where we achieve all the success we dream about. Some build a bridge between these two lives. Here are three short stories of success that seem to have very little in common:

1. For Amy Cuddy, the Excellence Habit came after a bad car accident. At age nineteen she was thrown out of a vehicle and rolled several times. She woke up in the hospital with a severe head injury. As a result, her IQ had dropped by two standard deviations, and she had been withdrawn from college. This was very traumatic for Amy because she identified with being very smart. She had been called "gifted" as a child. So she tried to go back and was told she was not going to be able to finish

college! There are other things she could do, she was told, but college was not going to work out. She really struggled with that. When her core identity was taken from her, it was the worst possible feeling.

As Amy felt overwhelmingly helpless, the one thing she could do was work. So she worked, and worked, and worked, and got a lucky break and back into college. Then she worked more, and eventually, Amy graduated from college. It took her four years longer than her peers. According to her Wikipedia page today, Amy Cuddy is an "American social psychologist known for her research on stereotyping and discrimination, emotions, power, nonverbal behavior, and the effects of social stimuli on hormone levels." She teaches at Harvard, and the video of her 2012 TED talk on body language has the second-highest number of all-time views on TED.com. Amy's story is extraordinary because when faced with seemingly insurmountable obstacles, she chose to follow her mission. To use the popular metaphor from the book *Who Moved My Cheese,* she chose to move her own cheese. Amy chose to keep working when there was no realistic hope she could get back what she had lost. Even when she believed she didn't belong in academia, Amy kept going.

2. For Jia Jiang, the path to the Excellence Habit started with a dream to become the next Bill Gates. In 2012, four days before his first child was born, Jiang, thirty-one, quit his corporate job at Dell. He started working full-time on his start-up. Jia had an agreement with his wife that she would support the family for six months. After that, he needed to get another job. About five months later, a major investor rejected Jia's business. This really crushed the young CEO. Jia felt as though he had been dumped. He hated the rejection, and he hated how much it hurt. So, Jia decided to study rejection to learn how to withstand it better. He devised a plan to get rejection from strangers so he could gradually "toughen up." Jia felt he needed to acquire this skill in order to be successful as an entrepreneur. To his surprise, instead of rejecting him, many of the odd requests he made of total strangers were accepted. For instance, he got to drive

a police car, fly a small airplane, make a PA announcement at Costco, and play soccer in a random homeowner's backyard.

Time and again, people said yes to Jia's unusual requests. He began making videos of his encounters and documented the surprising reactions. His plan was to get a no one hundred times in one hundred days to beat his fear of rejection. In November 2012, on his third day, he asked a Krispy Kreme manager to make him a set of doughnuts in the shape and colors of the Olympic Rings in fifteen minutes. His plan was to get another rejection. Instead, Jia got the doughnuts. The video of his failed attempt to get a no has more than five million views. As of 2015, Jia Jiang is a successful entrepreneur, published author, and public speaker. His story is inspiring because Jia faced his worst fears, took action to conquer them, and learned from the experience. Somewhere along the way of making his awkward requests, Jia gained authentic confidence, detached himself from the results, and turned rejection into an opportunity.

3. For Marco Morawec, the Excellence Habit became a key component of his new venture strategy. In 2013, together with fellow coder Ken Mazaika, Marco decided to teach beginners how to code a complete web app in one weekend. It was a bold idea, never done before. The two engineers called it "The Firehose Weekend." Their ambition, as declared on their site, was to "teach what matters and to condense at least five times the amount of comparable self-guided learning into each session." The focus was on the most important skills needed to build and deploy high-quality web applications.

After deciding on the idea, Marco and Ken started coding the website for their project. Then, it hit them. What if nobody wanted to pay for this kind of breakneck-pace learning? All their work on coding the website and preparing a curriculum would be wasted. Marco realized something else, too. As soon as they agreed on the idea, they went for what they knew how to do — coding. The idea to ask strangers to pay them for training was scary. This is when Marco realized that to succeed, they needed to operate outside their comfort zone. The two partners agreed on two principles. First, whatever they offered had to have a price. Second, they needed to do things that felt scary. So they stopped coding a new site and set up an online form with a "buy" button. The price of admission was $200, with an early-bird special of $100. Although it scared them, Marco and Ken did the logical thing. The best way to know whether someone would buy their course was to offer it for sale. When their first offering was fully subscribed in a couple of weeks, they were thrilled and terrified at the same time. They had a short time to figure out a curriculum and a place to teach. The first Firehose Weekend was a success. Three years later, Marco and Ken have run events from Boston and New York to Honolulu. Marco's story is enlightening because he realized that success would be outside his comfort zone and had the courage to act upon this. "A life worth living is spent outside your comfort zone!" became Marco's favorite sentence and a maxim he strives to apply relentlessly to this day.

What the stories of Amy, Jia, and Marco tell us is that even in adverse circumstances we can still find our way to success. We all face outside barriers, misfortunes, and obstacles in our lives. Most of us also struggle with internal resistance, procrastination, and distractions. To conquer these, often all we need is a small idea and the courage and tenacity to see it through. Whether it was finishing college after a head injury, overcoming fear of rejection, or choosing to follow our idea outside our comfort zone, in every case success followed.

However, many of us still remain feeling stuck. We live with this vague, gnawing sensation that "there should be something more." Doubt creeps into our hearts. Can we do this? Are we made from the same cloth? If yes, what is the line that still separates us from "them"? From the Amys and Jias and Marcos of the world?

Part of the problem is this: We believe that as adults we are entitled to comfort. We have completed all tests and exams and school is out forever. We graduated, and it is now time to live. We can relax, get a regular paycheck, and get to enjoy life for a change. It is good to be comfortable. This includes avoiding conflict or rejection as much as possible. This means giving in to our internal resistance or accepting our circumstances. If our paycheck doesn't allow us to drive the car that we want, then let's calculate what we can afford. We settle one step at a time. We call it "compromise," we call it "prudence," and we call it "realistic." We choose words that look good so we can feel comfortable with our choices. We do this to remove ourselves from the feeling of responsibility for our own less-than-100-percent decisions. What is worse — we don't even see this "comfortable adult" as a problem. We want to be a comfortable adult. So, we make comfort a habit.

Deep down we are aware of this problem. Kind of. If we do exceptional work, we have to move up, right? It is what we believe, and this conviction does not contradict our comfortable adult choice. We believe that all we have to do is work hard, do a great job, and it will happen. Somehow life owes us this. Oftentimes, during our honeymoon at a new job, this blind belief is rewarded. We bust our chops, we get recognized, and we get a pat on the back. It is this pat on the back that changes our attitude from blind faith to justified belief. Our idea that hard work pays off is proven correct, so we place more trust in the system. When what we think is true turns out to be true, we trust ourselves all the more. And we never revisit our comfortable adult choice.

One of the sources of success is our ability to change. It is our ability to recognize when it matters and take active steps to adjust, to move our own cheese. This is how we succeed — no matter what we define success to be. We succeed by learning to use "uncomfortable" and live with it, not by avoiding it.

The Excellence Habit is biography of an idea, and the idea is simple. The main source of success is excellence, and excellence depends more on our internal circumstances. Grit, determination, and the discipline to put in the hard work as a matter of habit, and not a matter of need, are crucial. And, because human psychology is so complicated, we have a hard time using rationally what we know about ourselves in order to build excellence as a habit.

This challenge is rooted in the fact that we already have a basic understanding about psychology. We all have experienced a wide range of emotions, from bliss to terror to enchantment. We all have felt inspired or intimidated by events. We have exercised self-control and discipline, or failed to do so. As we've grown out of childhood we have automated our days and we have automated our ways. Our decision-making is guided, and, more often than not, misguided by habits, which are based on biases. We build habits centered on irrational beliefs. Sometimes, human lives hang in the balance because of these biases. Findings from dozens of scientists around the world point to the inevitable conclusion that our minds, despite their powerful analytical capabilities, are also deeply flawed. We have evolved to make our brains happy. Ironically, for a fulfilling life we should accept the opposite. Jumping out of a perfectly good airplane, when our brain is screaming, "Stop!" is sometimes exactly what we should do. This is the idea. We have to master our ability to deal with adversity and to use it. A fulfilling life requires embracing rather than running from difficulty. The best way to do this is to discover and build our own Excellence Habit.

Success and excellence are often used as interchangeable synonyms, but they are not the same. We assume those who succeed did it because of the excellence of their work. We also believe that those who are committed to excellence will sooner or later succeed. There is, however, an important distinction between success and excellence. Success is often defined and measured against a set of goals. For instance, personal success often includes having a good family, nice house in a good neighborhood, stable career, etc. Professional success is mostly about achieving ever-higher business goals. In most cases, we measure success against the amount of social influence, recognition, and money we obtain. Success is about results. Excellence, on the other hand, is about the process. It is about how we do the work. It is about how much we do every day. It is about the road we take to reach our destination. What principles and habits did we apply to achieve success? How did we use our circumstances and our social and business networks to get where we needed to go? How were we changed, and how did we change others, while working on our goals? Are we happy about these changes? Are the others happy? What did we learn? What did we teach? In a way, excellence is a lot more than success and it is a lot more personal.

We focus on and dedicate our lives to success. Excellence may or may not be on our mind. We try to improve, and assume this will eventually lead to excellence. But let's consider for a bit a life dedicated to excellence. Let's look at the history and definitions of this term. The ancient Greeks had the concept of *arête*, which translates to outstanding "fitness for purpose." It appears in the works of Aristotle and Homer, and it basically means excellence of any kind. This includes moral virtue. The victorious warriors on the battlefield show *arête,* and so does Penelope for staying faithful to her husband Odysseus. The notion of excellence is essentially the fulfillment of purpose or function: the act of living up to our full potential. The idea of *arête* is often associated with courage and bravery but also with effectiveness. The person of *arête* uses all they've got — their courage, strength, and brains to achieve the best results possible. In some texts, *arête* is directly linked to knowledge as the highest virtue. All other human abilities are derived from our central capacity for knowledge. The Greek goddess that personified *arête* was called Harmonia.

So how does one achieve excellence? From ancient Greece to modern science, there seems to be one common theme. The most important way to achieve excellence is through practice. We hear that talent is 99 percent hard work. We talk about the ten-thousand-hour rule — the amount of practice needed to achieve great success in any field. In other words, we talk about building a habit. But is practice enough? Can we achieve excellence by simply repeating certain routines enough times? What if we were repeating it wrong from the beginning? So practice is important, but the gospel of the ten-thousand-hour rule is only half true. You can't get benefits from simple mechanical repetition. You need to bring your mind in on the action and make yourself work on adjusting your execution over and over to improve and get closer to your goal. This is a kind of smart practice and it needs to include a feedback loop that helps you see errors and correct them.

The good news is that our brains are really good at building routines. This is the first stage of excellence — the initial learning. We often get very excited at the beginning. Building an initial set of skills is a lot of fun. I have seen this time and again with my ten-year-old daughter. She starts a new activity like piano lessons or karate. With great excitement she learns the initial skill set. Then, she overcomes a great challenge like learning to play the *Frozen* theme song, or earning an orange belt. Then, after a few quick months the practice is no longer new. It gets boring. Eventually, she no longer wants to do it. In her brain the routine of doing the same thing over and over has become exhausting, frustrating, and undesirable. Her attention drifts during practice and the results are less and less satisfying.

When our attention drifts during practice, our brains only access what we already know. When we are not fully present the conscious brain does not engage. How can it? We are using it for daydreaming, or for thinking about vacation, or something else. At that moment, we engage only the learned experience, which is already automated in our subconscious minds. The process to rewire the relevant circuitry and improve the particular routine is absent. No change occurs, and the practice is all but wasted. This process, however, is über-important. It is the second and more important stage on the path to excellence. To become really good at something, we need to build a habit of paying attention while doing the boring practice stuff. The hard part is keeping the focus on how to make the small changes, the improvements in what we already know. These are the small steps that bring us closer to perfection. A life of excellence, therefore, is a life of paying attention and a life of deliberate, continuous change.

The need for continuous change is at the center of the idea of the Excellence Habit, and it also might be the hardest one to accept. In pursuit of this fundamental idea, I will take you on a journey over the skies of New York to learn how supreme excellence saved a damaged airplane full of passengers. I am going to introduce you to three fascinating principles I call The Iceberg Principle, The Law of Not Selling Out, and The Journey Mindset. We will revisit the famous Princeton Theological Seminary experiment to examine how the Good Samaritan relates to the power of context. I will tell you more about Amy Cuddy, and how she was able to wipe her inner graffiti and change her inner context to succeed. I will take you on a trip with the founder of Phunware, a successful tech start-up in

Austin, Texas, to understand how to build an Excellence Habit in an organization and make it stick.

The point of all this is to answer two simple questions that are at the heart of what we would all like to accomplish as professionals, parents, marketers, businesspeople, artists, and entrepreneurs. Why do we so often need to compel ourselves to do the right thing, and find it hard to follow the path to a life we want? What can we do to deliberately start and build a fulfilling life?

ONE

THE THREE RULES OF EXCELLENCE:

Within two minutes of takeoff, US Airways Flight 1549 lost both its engines. At an altitude of 2,818 feet, the aircraft hit a flock of Canadian geese and started to lose airspeed while still climbing. At that moment, Captain Chesley B. "Sully" Sullenberger took the controls over from First Officer Jeffrey Skiles, and the crew started exploring options for emergency landing. The date was January 15, 2009, and there were 150 passengers and five crewmembers on board. Nobody knows exactly how many options went through Captain Sully's mind at that moment. His years of service as a fighter pilot, airline pilot, safety expert, and a glider pilot certainly played a big role in what happened in the next three minutes. In a calm tone of voice and with brief statements, Captain Sully informed ground control about the aircraft's situation and requested emergency assistance. The controllers in the tower quickly offered a few options. In a concise manner, the captain rejected returning to LaGuardia or going to Newark. "We'll be in the Hudson!" is the last we hear from the recording of that radio exchange.

As the aircraft started losing altitude, the crew realized they could not reach the nearest airfield. So, Captain Sully turned the nose south, glided over the Hudson, and ditched the plane off Midtown Manhattan near the Intrepid Sea, Air, and Space Museum. About three minutes after losing power, they came to a stop in the river and everyone evacuated to safety. No lives were lost. National Transportation Safety Board member Kitty Higgins described the feat as "the most successful ditching in aviation history." The incident came to be known as the "Miracle on the Hudson."

Since then, when boarding a plane I often wonder: to what extent are the pilots capable of the same fast and effective decision making that saved the lives of everybody that morning over

Manhattan? Is Captain Sully a rare type of pilot, or are most of them qualified and prepared for extraordinary actions when needed? Can the aviation industry bottle Captain Sully and make him available in every cockpit? Can his excellence be learned? Can it be taught?

When examining human excellence, psychologists focus on understanding exceptional achievement in domains such as science, art, or sports. Some focus on natural talent, others on intensive training and practice. Then there are those who examine excellence as a product of context. For those supporting the nurture argument, it is all about exceptional performance training, deliberate practice, and a precocious involvement and commitment to a specific domain. The nurture fans believe that anyone can make it, and all they really need is hard and smart work. Regardless of context, personality traits, or upbringing, anyone can succeed with the right training. This is fully in line with the American fascination with the underdog. The notion that we were all created equal has taken root in our public discourse and has powerful implications socially, politically, on a personal level, and in our educational system. Popular culture reinforces these ideas with potent stories. From *Rocky* and *The Silence of the Lambs*, to *Avatar* and *The Girl with the Dragon Tattoo*, we follow and care about the journey of an unlikely hero who overcomes huge obstacles. Mainstream media reinforces this idea, too. We are accustomed to reading all about Bill Gates, Steve Jobs, Mark Zuckerberg, or Malala Yousafzai. They all achieved their status, fortune, and fame with tons of hard work and by overcoming unusually hard circumstances.

What is interesting about the nurture argument is that it is a relatively modern occurrence. Up until a few short decades ago, people were not expected to achieve much unless they were from the right caste, the right college, or born with the right title. In some countries you had to be a member of the Communist Party. We are now mostly done with the caste systems. There are fewer social barriers than ever, and this has increased our expectations. Never before have expectations been so high about what humans can achieve in their lives. The president of the United States is African American, the CEO of Microsoft is Indian-born, and rapper Dr. Dre sold his headphones company to Apple for $3 billion. We are told from many sources that anyone can achieve anything. This spirit of equality is a beautiful idea. Everybody now wears jeans and a T-shirt, yet deep, real inequalities remain. We are made to feel that if we have a bright idea, a garage or office, and work very, very hard, we can all become like Bill Gates or Steve Jobs. In reality—it is more likely to be hit by a lightning or win the lottery. Yet, the notion persists.

The second and perhaps more interesting fact about these high expectations is that we now officially live in the age of meritocracy. Politicians on the left and right, educators and social influencers agree that it is a good idea, and we should make our society more meritocratic. In other words, if you've got talent, energy, and skill, nothing should hold you back. You will get to the top. It is a logical, beautiful idea. If you deserve "it," you will get "it." There are a few problems with this idea. For one, if we truly believe in it, by implication the opposite must be true as well. Those who deserve to get to the bottom will get to the bottom and stay there. In other words, your position in life is merited and deserved. As a result, failure is much more harsh, personal, and devastating. It is almost presumed to be deliberate. It is curious how language has evolved to reflect this change in attitude. If we met a poor person a hundred years ago, we would likely call them unfortunate. Back then, we would describe them as someone who did not have enough fortune, who was not lucky enough. Nowadays, we would not be surprised to hear someone at the bottom of society be called a loser. I think we can all agree that there is a big difference between unfortunate and a loser. As a society we have evolved to believe less in God and more in ourselves. We are in the driver's seat of our lives, and, therefore, we own both success and failure. On a personal level, this has made it more difficult to feel good about our current level of success. By accepting the idea that we could achieve anything, we have increased the pressure on ourselves to do so. Paradoxically, this makes it more difficult to reach our goals.

There is more than one way to achieve excellence. Those who support the nature argument focus on cognitive, motivational, affective, and personality characteristics, as well as contextual elements. They believe that enhanced learning experiences and supportive environments are crucial factors in the process of excellence. While there is no sharp distinction between the two camps, nature versus nurture is a debate with passionate supporters on both sides. There are no apparent "winners." When we consider the power of context, it becomes even more difficult to offer clear-cut answers. Yet, on a personal level, there is an easy choice. When we want to reach higher we cannot do much about our nature. We are who we are — born with a predetermined collection of genes. We have our particular history, our upbringing, and our education. They are in the past and we cannot change them. We can't do much about luck either, other than prepare for it. At the end of the day, all we can really affect is ourselves. We can choose to practice more, practice better, and always do the right thing. When we find the way to build ourselves up, we hope our nature finds a way to adjust and our luck follows. This is why we say that great people create their circumstances. It is not because they have some magical powers to influence the world around them in a secret way. It is because they have built the habit to work and excel while others are just comfortable with the status quo. Excellence, therefore, is a function of the people who choose it, the preparation itself, and the principles that apply to this preparation. And when excellence happens, it is because all these agents of change have converged. These agents of change I call the Iceberg Principle, the Law of Not Selling Out and the Journey Mindset.

THE ICEBERG PRINCIPLE

Although we often forget it, Thomas Edison did not invent the concept of the light bulb. In fact, electric lights already existed on a streetlight scale by the time he came up with his version. In 1802, more than seventy years before Edison, a British inventor named Humphry Davy created the first electric light. Sir Davy was a chemist and is credited with discoveries of the elemental nature of chlorine and iodine. His lamp was called the carbon arc lamp and was used in coalmines. After 1850, in the United States, there were attempts to produce arc lamps commercially, but the lack of a constant electricity supply thwarted this effort.

Over the next decades, other inventors also came up with light bulbs, but none of the designs was commercially viable. In 1850, English physicist Joseph Wilson Swan created a light bulb by enclosing carbonized paper filaments in a glass bulb. By 1878, Swan had improved on his design and demonstrated his new electric lights in Newcastle, England.

When, in 1879, Edison created his light bulb, it was the first that proved practical, and affordable, for home illumination. The trick had been to choose a durable, yet inexpensive, filament. This detail alone took quite a few attempts to get it right. Edison experimented with several materials for the light bulb element ranging from various types of metals to beard hair. The element is the part of the bulb that glows or incandesces when the electricity is passing through. Carbonized thread proved to be initially successful.

Not happy with a light bulb that worked for about forty hours, the famous inventor continued to experiment with other materials for the bulb element. Edison and his assistants tested more than six thousand plant materials as possible options. Ultimately, carbonized bamboo from Japan proved the right choice. When cut to the proper dimensions and carbonized, the bamboo incandesced for more than 1,200 hours. The material also became a convenient choice because it helped Edison bypass some lawsuits involving other inventors. A practical, commercially viable electric lamp was born.

This part of the story is common knowledge. When Edison lit up his laboratory and office before Christmas of 1879, he was looking at the same new bulb as everyone else. But what he saw was different. Edison was looking at the result of more than six thousand tests. Can you imagine the feeling? One successful design came after thousands of unsuccessful ones. The inventor was also looking at the first commercially viable product for home illumination and he knew it. His invention was going to change how we lived and how we worked. This goal drove his relentless experimentation. Edison didn't care if he had to conduct six thousand, twelve thousand, or fifty thousand tests. He probably was not concerned that he didn't have the first-mover advantage, or all the patents, or the necessary technology. He didn't worry about commercial production and distribution. Edison kept going till he had an inexpensive, long-lasting electrical light bulb.

In his own way, he was aware of the concept that Seth Godin so eloquently expressed: "No one knows the right answer, no one knows precisely what will happen, no one can produce the desired future, on demand." What Edison knew and applied as a habit in his work was the Iceberg Principle.

The Iceberg Principle simply says that the majority of our efforts are invisible to the eye. Just as the majority of the ice mass of an iceberg is underwater, so is the majority of hard work it takes to build lasting excellence habits. An important aspect of this principle is that often the effort we make is meant to achieve other goals. We train for one field, and then it turns out this also prepares us for another. Edmund Hillary trained as a boxer, and later the strength he built made him suitable for mountaineering and eventually allowed him to be the first man on Everest. In his childhood, Ernest Hemingway hated going to cello practice but later admitted the music lessons were useful to his writing. Captain Sully was certified as a glider pilot, and this later allowed him to ditch a commercial airliner in the Hudson, with zero casualties. As Steve Jobs used to say: you can only connect the dots looking backward.

Risk, adversity, and patience are three key concepts when we think about the Iceberg Principle. Risk is often perceived, not necessarily real. Not every black swan, or worst-case scenario that we imagine, will actually materialize and destroy our lives. Adversity and patience are related. We can often feel the fight-or-flight urge when, in fact, the most proper response would be to focus on the job. When we feel inpatient, it is often because of the fear that we are missing out. The fear that if we are not achieving anything today, then we are paying a high opportunity cost. The world will pass us by. A part of us knows that this is not true, but it is hard to overcome the feeling.

So what do we do with the Iceberg Principle? How do we make it useful to our everyday lives? Is it relevant to our ability to compel ourselves to walk the path to the life we want? Yes, of course, it is. The metaphor of the iceberg is not new or earth-shattering. It is just a good way to remind ourselves that most big accomplishments happen after tons of hard work. As Seth Godin put it: we need to show up every day with our best work and not hold back. This is one of those small adjustments in our mindset that will help make a big difference in our lives. If we want to deliberately start and build a fulfilling life, we have to remember the Iceberg Principle. Once we make this choice, and it is a choice, it will be easier to accept those days when we seemingly achieve nothing. It will be easier to focus on improving. It will be easier to understand that even when we don't see a purpose in our hard work, it is still better to do the work than to give in to inner doubts and resistance.

THE LAW OF NOT SELLING OUT

Will the choice of the Iceberg Principle be enough? Of course not. Hard work needs to be matched with appropriately high goals and higher standards. Edison did not compromise with a forty-hour bulb. He kept going till his product could last at least twelve hundred hours. This is an example of the principle I call the Law of Not Selling Out. Certainly, Edison could have been commercially successful if the bulb lasted six hundred hours. One might even argue that this would have been a good way for him to make even more money. Yet, Edison believed there were certain standards he couldn't break. Compromise is good when our in-laws are about to visit for the holidays, or when an erratic driver cuts us off in traffic. However, there are times when we need to stick to our guns.

The Law of Not Selling Out says that no matter what the circumstances, we keep intact our core values, beliefs, and principles. This is central to understanding excellence. When we are committed to building an Excellence Habit, it is critical to stick to our principles even as our goals may change. Excellence is fitness for a purpose and we need to remember this purpose. Will there be setbacks? Certainly. Will there be times when we feel overwhelmed by circumstances? Most likely. Yet, when we are committed to excellence, we keep our principles intact. Remember: success most often happens on the outside, while excellence always happens on the inside first. As Edmund Hillary said, it is not the mountain that we conquer, but ourselves. Can we choose to climb a different mountain? Yes. Our purpose will be most rewarding when it fits well with who we are. The "who we are" portion is the more challenging one.

THE JOURNEY MINDSET

When Kerry M. Healey was sworn into office as the lieutenant governor of Massachusetts on January 2, 2003, she assumed her responsibilities with a clear agenda on day one. Part of this agenda was laws that curbed gang violence, enhanced witness safety, expanded the rights of those wrongfully convicted, advanced technology to track sex offenders, curbed substance abuse, strengthened law enforcement's ability to combat opioid abuse, and expanded protection from sex offenders. This is a serious list for day one. In an interview in 2007, Healey cited her greatest accomplishment as lieutenant governor as the work that she did to ensure the passage of Melanie's Law. This is a 2005 Massachusetts law that strengthened penalties for drunk driving in order to keep repeat offenders off the road. The result was a 44 percent drop in repeat drunk-driving offenses in its first year.

These outstanding results were not accidental. The success of Kerry Healey as an elected official was the tip of the iceberg. To get there, she had spent years of building an Excellence Habit as a consultant to the US Department of Justice on criminal justice issues. For a decade, she was looking at drug crimes, child abuse and neglect, gang violence, domestic violence, and recidivism. In her own words:

"At the end of that time I had a very good, broad knowledge on social dysfunction, but I had no real way of having any impact on solving these problems. So what I decided to do was to run for office."

What propelled her run was that reservoir of knowledge, which she was not able to get into the public forum in any other way. Running for office also took time. It would be four years before she became an elected official.

To learn more about Kerry Healey's principles, I reached out for an interview in person. As of 2015, Dr. Kerry Healey is in her third year as President of Babson College — the number one school in Entrepreneurship for nineteen consecutive years. Her office on campus is at the top of the Horn Library building. One needs to go through a couple of library levels brimming with young students to reach the relatively small office area.

We talk about the Iceberg Principle first:

"When I became lieutenant governor in 2002, I had a fully- formed agenda. This is a spectacular asset. So many politicians who come into office are like Robert Redford in the movie *The Candidate,* who says "Now what?" While four years in office may seem like a long time, within a legislative environment it is extremely short. So if you don't walk in on day one and know precisely what you want to do, then it is very unlikely that you are going to succeed."

When we discuss her personal Excellence Habits, Dr. Healey said that her ability to deal with ambiguity for very long periods of time is probably more important than self-discipline. This is critical when working toward long-term goals. We need to understand and accept that things may go in entirely different directions than what we were preparing for. Dr. Healey also speaks about the ability to be vulnerable:

"Even if I fail, and fail very publicly, I don't take it very personally. As long as I have put forward my best effort, and as long as I believe in what I was doing, then I am not very concerned about public judgment."

This one statement conveys the core of the Law of Not Selling Out. In any field and endeavor, we are the sum of all our preparation. The results we get also depend on level of effort, context, and circumstances. Despite our best hard work, we will sometimes face situations that push us in a different direction. Sometimes adversity will disguise itself in the form of success, or worse — the desire for success. We will face the comfortable adult setting. Dr. Healey moved on after her term as lieutenant governor, partially because she had accomplished a big part of her agenda. What she had learned from ten years of consulting on criminal justice issues had resulted in positive change on a large scale. "Not selling out" applies to principles as well as money. If you really do believe in the principles you are fighting for, if you believe in the value of what you have to offer, then you are not going to feel uncomfortable about a loss. If someone compromised their beliefs in order to succeed, and then they failed, they would feel very bad.

When we understand and apply consistently the Law of Not Selling Out, we gain the power to transfer our experience and values across fields. Today, Dr. Healey has brought her beliefs and values to Babson College. There is, again, an agenda from day one:

"The school has a very clear mission, and it is to educate entrepreneurial leaders who create economic and social value everywhere. There is a global aspect to the mission, there is a social benefit piece, and there is an educational piece. In a world where entrepreneurship is becoming a major force for lifting people out of poverty and empowering people who have nothing but their own initiative, this is what Babson needs to do."

A key notion that drives this mission is that it will help redefine the purpose of business in society. The idea is that Babson graduates will view the creation of economic and social value as a simultaneous process, as opposed to separate or sequential. Putting together profit and social benefit is a powerful differentiator for an educational institution. It is also very much in line with the expectations of the students who choose the business school.

In a time when there is a global debate about the morality of capitalism, this is a winning approach to teaching the next generation of economic leaders. Kerry Healey came from a background in criminal justice issues, government, and now education. As a generalist who actively chooses a new field of study every two years, she can see the connections between these fields. Criminal issues are connected to health and economic ones, and socially responsible entrepreneurship can provide answers to all of these.

Problem solving on this level can occur when the third principle of excellence is present. This third principle I call the Journey Mindset. This is a small change in our mindset that over time can make a big difference in our lives. It is a mindset that works for people like Kerry Healey, who continues her service in big and meaningful ways. It also works for anyone who is starting out. As a young entrepreneur, Jia Jiang felt the pain of failure when his first venture was denied investment. But he decided to interpret this painful setback as a step on his journey, and use it for personal growth. For him the payoff was relatively quick. He dared himself to ask for rejection, and in the process he not only toughened himself but also found success. This is a powerful example of how the Journey Mindset can transform someone's life. The more natural response for anyone in Jia's shoes would have been to block the painful memory of the rejection and to move on. Who needs to be reminded daily about a sore stage in their lives? However, when we accept that each stage in our life is a necessary part of our journey, then we would be able to seek and find meaning and benefit in everything we do. Will there be times when we are forced outside of our comfort zones? It is practically guaranteed. Is this a bad thing? Only if we lack the Journey Mindset.

Tenacity, self-discipline, and grit are the common denominators for the three principles of excellence. We need the drive to keep going even when most of our efforts remain invisible below the surface—a part of the iceberg, which, one day, will be our success. We need the self-discipline to not sellout, not go for the easy win, but stick to our principles and values when it matters. We need the determination to see everything in our lives as part of our unique journey.

The three principles of the Excellence Habit—the Iceberg Principle, the Law of Not Selling Out, and the Journey Mindset, offer a way of making sense of our own path to success and fulfillment. They provide us with direction for how to go about discovering and building excellence as part of our daily lives. The rest of this book will take these ideas and apply them to other situations from the world around us. How do these three principles help us understand compassion, the power of context, or fighting crime in the New York subway system? The answers will be worthwhile and may surprise you.

TWO

THE TENNIS BALL EFFECT

In the final moments of the Woody Allen movie *Match Point,* the main character throws some key evidence against him in the river Thames. He is a tennis player who married into a rich family, had an affair, and committed murder. While getting rid of the evidence, a ring slides out, and, instead of flying into the water, hits the railing, bounces off in the air, and falls back onto the sidewalk. The protagonist doesn't notice. The moment is just like earlier in the movie, when a tennis ball hits the net, bounces up in the air, and creates a few moments of suspense for players and audience alike. Is it going to go over and register as a point, or fall back and become an unforced error? By a clever twist of plot, so typical of Woody Allen's mastery, the ring ends up saving the main character from jail, but not from his conscience. The whole story is a witty take on the premise that small changes in our environment can have a big and often unexpected effect on our fate. The bigger question is can our environment influence our behavior, trump our character? Our personalities are made of our beliefs, principles, and habits. To what extent are we in charge of these?

To start answering these questions, let's revisit the Good Samaritan story from the Bible. A man gets beaten up badly and is left by the side of the road. A priest and then a Levite walk by without helping the one in need. The third person to walk by is a Samaritan, who stops and helps the fallen man. The story is an example of how the virtues that the religious leaders preached were not something they followed themselves.

In 1971, two researchers at Princeton Theological Seminary conducted a social experiment that re-created the situation from the Good Samaritan story. The experiment included a few additional situational variables. Forty students were asked to complete a questionnaire, and then were told to go to another building to give a talk. Half were supposed to talk about jobs suitable for seminary graduates, and the rest were to talk about the parable of the Good Samaritan. Before moving on to the next building, different groups of students were given different information regarding their time constraints. Some were told they were late and so they needed to hurry. Others were told they could potentially be late and so also had to make haste. A third and final group was told they had a few extra minutes and so had no need to rush. Once outside, without knowing that it was part of the experiment, the participants had to pass by an actor who was on the ground and clearly in distress. Who do you think stopped and offered help?

Ironically, a person in a hurry was far less likely to help someone in distress, even if he was about to speak about the parable of the Good Samaritan. One of the participants literally stepped over the victim on his way to the next building. The researchers found that the topic selection did not have much influence on behavior. Despite the expected cognitive conditioning, it didn't matter whether the participants were going to talk about vocations or about the parable of the Good Samaritan. The one variable that significantly affected behavior was the "hurry factor." The more hurried the participants were, the less help they offered. Only 10 percent of those in the "high hurry" category offered aid to the suffering actor. Compare this to the 63 percent of the "low hurry" subjects who stopped to offer help. Clearly, the distraction and the pressure of the imminent public speaking could have caused the students to be unaware of the suffering actor. An exit questionnaire, however, confirmed that most participants were aware of the actor as "someone possibly in need of help."

One of the paradoxes this study raises is that all too quickly we apply dismissive labels to people as a result of their actions or lack of actions. For instance, most of us assume without second thought that a seminary student would always be compassionate. So when one of these students steps over a body on his way to give a talk on the Good

Samaritan story, this is shocking. We tend to ignore the power of context, which is so significant in our behavior. All too often we fail to stop and think before being too hard on ourselves as well as others. And once we judge a behavior, it is that much easier to move to the next step and judge people. We fail to appreciate that as with many things in life, the tennis ball of what we do will bounce off the net of circumstances and fly up in the air. Whether we score, or have an unforced error, is often beyond our immediate control.

What does this have to do with our path to excellence? How can this power of context help us become better? For starters, this is an important reminder to let go of things beyond our control. We can somewhat improve our circumstances by careful planning. However, when the tennis ball hits the net and bounces up in the air, it is already outside of our control. The variables that we can control the most are our thoughts, emotions, and actions. At least in theory. We are always supposed to have the choice how to respond to any situation we encounter. Sometimes, however, situations develop quickly, or in a seemingly threatening manner. A stranger confronts us on the street and asks for money. The boss of our boss stops by to demand a report we are not ready with. We are told we are late and need to hurry up. These are the fastballs, the stressful situations, which often drive us to the evolutionary fight-or-flight response. This is powerful programming that we know well, and it is easy to follow. We are so used to having this response that even when everyday situations are not as threatening, our feeling of anxiety is as though they were.

The one stress factor that always reduces our choices and affects how we react is the availability of time. As the experiment at the seminary demonstrated, at any moment we are hurried, or feel hurried, we will exhibit a diminished ability to respond in line with our circumstances. Even when we encounter new, unfamiliar, and potentially dangerous circumstances, if we had plenty of time, we would have a better chance of self-control and adequate response. When time starts running out, so does our capacity for reaction, problem solving, and creativity. This is almost universal as a response to time pressure. Awareness and preparation, therefore, are critical to how well we perform when short on time. There are plenty of examples, where through extended practice, people develop the cool-under-pressure mindset. We can clearly see them in the NFL, for instance. Some clutch players perform better when the clock hits the two-minute warning, and others seem to falter. For anyone looking to build an Excellence Habit, this is a critical point, so let me say it one more time: Practice and how well we do under pressure are positively correlated. We have to keep reminding ourselves that the more we prepare, the better we will perform when it matters.

THE BROKEN WINDOWS OF OUR SOUL

In 1969, Stanford psychologist Philip Zimbardo arranged for two cars with no license plates to be placed unattended in the Bronx, New York, and Palo Alto, California. Within minutes of its abandonment, the car in the Bronx was attacked. The first vandals were a family: a father, mother, and a young son. They took the car's battery and radiator. Within twenty-four hours that car was stripped of everything of value. Then, the windows were smashed in, upholstery ripped apart, and the neighborhood kids started using it as a playground. At the same time, the car in Palo Alto remained untouched for more than a week. Then, Zimbardo deliberately took a hammer and smashed it. Soon after, people in Palo Alto also joined in the destruction. This experiment was used to examine what is known in criminology as the broken windows theory. Undesirable events like these can occur in any civilized community when the sense of mutual regard and civility are lowered by actions that suggest indifference. In other words, when a broken window is left broken, soon after someone will smash a second one, and in a short time the property will be vandalized. In an article in 1982, criminologists James Wilson and George Kelling argued that crime is the inevitable result of disorder.

Author Malcolm Gladwell took this idea one step further. In his book *The Tipping Point*, he argued that crime is contagious. It can start with a broken window and spread in the community like an epidemic. A feature in our environment can trigger the impetus to engage in certain kinds of behavior. One small issue in the context can lead to larger problems in society. After that article in 1982, the New York Transit Authority hired Kelling as a consultant, and he urged them to put the broken windows theory into practice. At that time in the 1980s, the New York subway system was not a safe place. Crime and destruction were prevalent. Based on Kelling's advice, management took steps to reclaim the subway system from vandals and criminals. Their weapon of choice? Paint brushes.

Instead of focusing on crime and subway reliability, the transit authority started by erasing and painting over the graffiti that covered the subway cars. In 1984, every single one of the six thousand cars in the New York subway system were covered with graffiti—top to bottom, inside and out. The theory was that if the Transit Authority created a different environment, this could reduce the undesirable behaviors. It was a clear message to the vandals and to the community at large. Each night the kids would spray-paint a new car and once they were done, workers with rollers would come out and paint it over. No car was allowed to leave the yard if still covered in graffiti.

A similar approach was undertaken to combat crime on the subway. Instead of focusing on the more serious offenses, transit police decided to crack down on fare-beating. At the time, an estimated seventeen thousand people a day entered the system without paying a token. The head of the transit police believed that like graffiti, fare-beating was a signal. It was a small expression of disorder that invited more serious transgressions. By 1994, the graffiti and fare-beating initiatives produced a drastic reduction in crime in the subway. The key lesson from these events is that the power of context is greater than we usually assume. We are more than just sensitive to changes in our environment. We are delicately fine-tuned to them. And even minor changes to our context can alter our oath to excellence in ways we could not have foreseen.

When we discuss the power of context and its role in building our Excellence Habit, the assumption is that all context is external. However, there is another kind that really matters. This is our internal context. On any given day, we wake up, and the stream of our consciousness starts and takes us through our morning routine. Without major changes, our mental state tends to become more and more habitual. If there were no outside disruptors, the trends in our lives become more clearly outlined. If we liked our first job, we tend to like the second one as well. If we were driven in college, we tend to become more ambitious in our careers. Within the context of our minds, we take the facts from our daily lives and process them against our personal history. With each day, any changes that we make are less and less noticeable. Based on our beliefs and values and on our environment, we create a mental context that allows us to feel more or less in control of our lives. Our mental state becomes a product of habit. We tend to have the same reaction to similar circumstances. And while we tend to spend a lot of time thinking about and noticing our external circumstances, we tend to pay little or no attention to our internal context. Our thoughts and our feelings often go on automatic. We rarely decide to "have a good day" regardless of the coming snowstorm and the dreaded month-end business review. On the contrary, we tend to anticipate and justify our bad moods based on the external context.

Just as with our external environment, our mental context is a major factor in the results we get. And just as with our external circumstances, our internal state can have "broken windows." From childhood trauma and bad experiences, to poor habits and wrong choices, we carry with us the luggage of our inner circumstances. And just as with the broken windows theory in criminology, we are exquisitely sensitive to minor changes in our internal context. Without noticing, we can be affected by a smell, a tune on the radio, or an old poster. An odd thought could pop up during a meeting at the office, and then we find ourselves drifting for fifteen minutes and missing important information. A full moon could trigger a sleepless night, which we try to correct the next day with extra coffee. These are all small sensory-triggered changes in our mental context that can end up having a big impact on our day. However, there is another class of inner context factors that are even more powerful in determining the kind of life we are going to have. These factors are our prevailing thoughts, beliefs, and values. This is what we tell ourselves on a daily basis, and what we tell ourselves in situations that matter. And what we tell ourselves sometimes comes from a single moment. One point in time can define our lives.

WIPING OUT OUR INNER GRAFFITI

For Amy Cuddy, that defining moment came when at age nineteen she was in a bad car crash. It landed her in the hospital. When she woke up, she had a severe head injury, and as a result she had been withdrawn from college. Her IQ had dropped significantly. Because she identified as being very smart, Amy was devastated. When you are called "gifted" as a child and then you can't even graduate from college, it's a real struggle. I can't imagine how a life-changing event like that would affect someone's mental state. What do you tell yourself when your core identity is taken away from you?

After years of hard work and getting a couple of lucky breaks, Amy managed to graduate from college. It took her four years longer than her peers. When she landed a job in academia, Amy had a mental context of "I don't belong here." Years of struggle and hard work without hope had created a complete lack of confidence. This mental frame was so strong that Amy had a recurring fear she would be exposed as a fraud and thrown out. During her first year working at Princeton, she needed to give a talk to a group of her peers. The night before the talk, she called her boss and told her she was quitting. Her mental context was in such a dire conflict with reality that she chose the basic flight response. Instead of going through with her assignment, she was ready to escape. Her boss convinced her to stay. "No, you are not quitting. If you feel you don't belong, you will go in and fake it!" her boss told her. With words to that effect, she successfully addressed Amy's mental context. If you feel like a fraud, then fake it. Accept yourself for who you believe you are and go do your job.

The ability to accept ourselves for who we believe we are is one of those major mental context factors that have the power to shape our lives. Some people are good at it. Others struggle. For most of us it starts at school. As we mature, we find a certain weirdness about ourselves that we prefer to keep private. Over time this becomes a habit, and then it becomes so automatic that we don't even think about it anymore. At school we learn to use social conventions to hide. We accept we are band geeks, or jocks, or bookworms, or outcasts. We know that these labels only define a small portion of who we are. But we use them as a camouflage, a protective mechanism. As we enter adulthood we might outgrow this, or we become too comfortable with the protection of the social label. So much so that we start to believe it. We tell ourselves stories that support this label. "Not bad for a band geek, but did I really deserve this promotion?" Talk about self-sabotaging mental context.

This is what happened with Amy Cuddy as well. She got so used to telling herself that she had a lower IQ that she failed to see how she had come back and earned her spot in academia. She was a smart kid again, but she didn't notice it. Or she noticed it, but she didn't believe it. Her mindset needed an adjustment. She needed to change her story from "I am not supposed to be here!" to "I belong here!" This was one of the big broken windows in her mental framework. This space in her inner context was covered with graffiti—top to bottom, inside and out. The graffiti of the impostor syndrome dominated her. The story of when and how she wiped these graffiti clean probably deserves a separate book. But one day Amy Cuddy realized she had changed her inner context.

It was years later during her first year teaching at Harvard. One of her students, who had not participated in class the whole year, came to Amy and told her, "I am not supposed to be here!"

At that moment Amy had an epiphany. She realized two things. First, it was "Oh, my gosh—I don't feel like that anymore!" She knew exactly what the student was talking about, and she was no longer under the spell of this broken window. The second thing she realized was, she knew exactly how to help her student.

"Yes, you are supposed to be here. And, tomorrow, you are going to fake it! You will go into the classroom and you will make the best comment ever."

And the next day in class, her student did exactly that—she raised her hand and made the best comment. Other students were leaning over to see if this really was the quiet one talking. Over time, that student made it a habit; she faked it till she became it.

CHANGING OUR BODIES TO CHANGE OUR MINDS

As of the time of this writing more than twenty-seven million people have seen Amy Cuddy tell her story in a 2012 TED talk, making it the second most watched TED video. At that time in 2012, she was working at Harvard and studying the connection between how we feel and our body language. She found out that, not surprisingly, when we feel powerful and confident we tend to expand our bodies and occupy as much of the real estate around us as possible. We stretch our hands and legs, raise our chin, and pump up our chest. When feeling powerless, the opposite happens. People tend to fold in, cross their hands and legs, and make themselves appear smaller than they are. There is a direct correlation between how we feel and the kind of nonverbal behavior we exhibit.

Then, Amy Cuddy asked an important question—is the opposite connection valid as well? She tested her hypothesis by examining the effect of high-power and low-power postures on a random group of people. The subjects were asked to take one of the poses for two minutes, and then they were asked a question about gambling. It is well documented that people who feel more powerful are more inclined to gamble. Another sign of feeling powerful and confident are higher testosterone levels and lower cortisol levels. High testosterone is a sure sign of power and confidence. Cortisol is also known as the stress hormone and associated with low power. So Amy also took saliva samples before and after the two minutes and compared them. The results were astonishing. Eight-six percent of the high-power-pose group were inclined to gamble versus just 60 percent for the low-power group. Further, those who stayed for two minutes in body postures associated with high power had an increase of their testosterone of about 20 percent. Those who were asked to assume the low-power pose experienced a decrease of about 10 percent. The high-power people had a decrease in cortisol of about 25 percent and the low-power people experienced a 15 percent increase. None of the participants were conditioned in any way and they did not know the goal of the study. So, in just two minutes we can experience these changes in attitude and body chemistry? We can start feeling assertive, confident, and comfortable or become really stress-reactive and feel shut down. This is major. It turns out small changes in our body language do have a significant effect on body chemistry and how we feel about ourselves. In other words, our bodies can and do change our minds in very specific ways.

The next question is this: Can power posing for a few minutes really change our lives in meaningful ways? Was it possible for someone like Jia Jiang to overcome his fear of rejection without doing one hundred rejection videos in one hundred days, but instead by simply incorporating some appropriate body-pose exercises? Is it possible for every one of us to reimagine and remake our future? To find answers, Amy and her team at Harvard tested the effect of nonverbal behavior in high-stress job-interview situations. They had high-power and low-power posers go on a mock job interview for five minutes where the interviewer gave them zero nonverbal feedback. A random group of people were asked to take on a high-power or low-power pose for two minutes and then interviewed with someone who stared back at them with a blank face — no emotion or reaction whatsoever. People hate this more than heckling and it is really stressful. After these interviews were videotaped, Amy's team asked a set of recruiters to look at the videos and select who they would hire. These recruiters were not aware of the setting of these interviews or the goal of the experiment. Although they were looking at a random group of people who went through identical interviews, all recruiters said they wanted to hire the high posers and rated them overall as better than the low posers.

Another interesting discovery from this experiment was that the content of their speech did not change as a result of the different poses. The posing affected the presence of the candidates. The power posers were described as "passionate," "enthusiastic," "captivating," "comfortable," "authentic," and "confident." This is what the posing influenced. The candidates were presenting the same verbal information, but they were more confident and "more themselves" as they were doing it. That made all the difference. This is big. Something as small and seemingly insignificant as taking on a certain posture for two minutes can change the outcome of important events like a job interview. Seriously?

So, it turns out there are small changes that we can make, which will help us move our cheese in a big way. Just two minutes of posing before an important meeting, presentation, or interview is really not much effort. Stage actors routinely practice similar techniques before show time. It is like using your body to speak your positive mantra and get yourself in the mode, which helps you communicate with presence and in a confident, authentic manner.

In one of her many interviews, charisma guru, consultant, and lecturer Olivia Fox Cabane tells the fable of a tiger who had a small enclosure in a zoo. The majestic animal used to pace back and forth from one end of the enclosure to the other till all the grass under his feet disappeared and turned into a path. Eventually, after some time, the tiger was moved to a new, much larger enclosure. However, he continued pacing approximately the same distance as in his old enclosure. For the rest of his days the tiger never ventured outside of his usual range despite his new, much larger space. "Don't be that tiger!" is the author's message. When there is new information that opens up new possibilities in your life, there is usually a price to pay. This price is getting out of your comfort zone. This is easier said than done. Fox Cabane knows this better than anyone. She teaches CEOs and leaders of billion-dollar organizations how to be better at the fine art of personal charisma and magnetism.

Imagine how hard it is for a smart, successful CEO to go out of her way to learn new skills. She needs to get outside her comfort zone just so she can achieve a little bit more. How do they do it and why? Why did Steve Jobs do it? He was successful, with a big ego and not a lot of charisma, initially. He worked hard at it. He built an attitude of excellence and then made it into a habit. Being comfortable was not a part of Steve Jobs' daily routine. He also did not expect or allow anyone working for him to be comfortable. This was his life philosophy. This is why he did it. He knew that to keep succeeding, he needed to keep improving. He affirmed the power of this principle with his famous closing advice to the graduating class at Stanford:

"Stay hungry. Stay foolish."

It is probably not a coincidence that Amy Cuddy's field of study deals with how our body language shapes who we are. She works on discovering how our body changes our minds, and how in turn our minds change our behavior. Amy Cuddy has built her Excellence Habit. To be where she is today, she invested tons of work, most of which was invisible, even to her. For years, there was no hope, yet she didn't sell out or give up. And she continues her journey by helping others find their way to a fulfilling life. Amy followed the three principles of excellence. And one of the key takeaways from her world-famous TED talk is this:

Small tweaks => BIG CHANGES.

THREE

REWRITING OUR STORY

In a memory experiment conducted by the University of Washington in 2001, participants recalled shaking hands with Bugs Bunny on their trip to Disneyland. Since Bugs Bunny is a Warner Bros character and is not featured at Disneyland, the study demonstrated how easy it was to plant false memories. Brain scientists know that our memory does not work like a video camera. Instead of "recording" and then "playing back" an event, when we recall a memory we get a mix between our current experiences, the reason for recalling the specific memory, and the memory itself.

A Northwestern University School of Medicine study published in the *Journal of Neuroscience* in 2014 described how specifically our mind can insert things from the present into memories from the past when they are retrieved. For instance, the memory of the thrill of that first kiss might very well be a mix of the actual memory and our current feelings toward the same person. Most people in happy relationships report the first kiss as an extra-special event — a central part of the treasure of the relationship coffers. However, what happens is that we are projecting our current feelings back to the original encounter. In essence, our memory reframes and edits events from our past in order to fit the story of our current world.

The lead author of the study, Donna Jo Bridge, points out that memory is designed to help us make good decisions in the moment. What is important right now can override and even delete and rewrite what was in the past. As part of our evolution, our memories have adapted to an ever-changing environment to help us deal with the present.

What are the implications of the fact that memory is not 100 percent reliable? Certainly, we can think again about all the eyewitness testimonies in the courtroom. How many cases are affected by testimony based on unreliable memories? Another example is advertising. If it was easy to convince us that we saw something that wasn't there, what other kind of brainwashing are we susceptible to? Perhaps many of us can find an answer to this by checking our closets for items we bought at some point and then forgot about.

So what can we do with this information if we want to build an Excellence Habit? How can we use the knowledge that our own memories give us a story, as opposed to the actual cold truth? Our own brains do this automatically to help us make better decisions in the present. Can we do the same? Can we use our minds deliberately to rewrite our own story, reframe our mental context, and ultimately change our lives? Absolutely. This is the only way it actually happens. Every person who has ever achieved deliberate change first made up their minds that they wanted change. The outcome may not always be what we imagined, or what we wanted. Sometimes, the change we initiate takes us to unexpected, or even undesirable places. We can only connect the dots of our story looking backward. And looking forward, there is almost no fate that we cannot change. How many first-time Oscar winners pointed out in their acceptance speech that the award was an impossible dream? So, if we want to deliberately build a more fulfilling life, we need to start imagining it first.

This leads us to the other source of stories that we have—our own imagination. We use imagination in our daily lives far more often than we think we do. Many people believe imagination is this big, special thing reserved for geniuses and creative people. For many, using imagination in our routine, daily lives is not required and can often be perceived as negative. For instance, daydreaming on the job is not a good thing, right? Especially if the quality of our work suffers as a result, and it makes us look bad. However, at some point we want to improve. We want to be better off, respected at work and among friends, and we want a sense of fulfillment.

How do we build a habit to think and act in a way that gives us these results?

To answer this question we will look closely at how our minds get addicted.

ADDICTED TO EXCELLENCE

So our emotions can be messy, our memories can serve us with "a story," and our brains get easily addicted. Brain scientists have established that we are all equipped with a special "rewards center" that selectively motivates us. Ideally, the motivated behaviors are ones that benefit us. There are the basic ones concerning food, shelter, care of our young, and procreation. Then there are the achievement motivators, which drive us to seek more complicated pleasurable experiences.

Scientists call this area in our brains the mesolimbic reward center. It is one of the four main dopamine pathways in the brain and a key detector of rewarding stimulus. It is, therefore, an important determinant of motivation and incentive. In simplistic terms, activation of this center tells us to repeat what we did to get that reward. It also tells the memory centers in the brain to pay particular attention to all features of that rewarding experience, so it can be repeated in the future. It is a very old pathway from an evolutionary point of view. The use of dopamine neurons to trigger behavioral responses to natural rewards is seen in worms and flies, which evolved one to two billion years ago.

One very interesting feature of this rewards center is that it is a bit like a power grid that can be tapped into, hacked, and even hijacked by external forces. When that happens, our rewards circuitry is used in the exact same way, only the rewards that are imprinted are not beneficial. When this imprinting of rewards that are no good overwhelms the brain rewards center, we see someone who is "addicted" to a substance or behavior.

One reason for addiction is the neural reward we get from the sense of belonging. Researchers have established that many of us get this sense from online interactions. In a study, Scott Caplan, a professor of communication at the University of Delaware, observed that people who prefer online social interactions over face-to-face ones also scored higher on compulsive Internet use and using the Internet to alter their moods. In many professions, we are faced with the inevitable reality that we spend more time connecting with people online than we do with people who are physically in our presence. If we add to this the time spent connecting with our favorite TV programs, we can see how overwhelmed our brains can be.

It is not all bad news. Research on the effect of TV, for instance, suggests that just thinking about our favorite TV show buffers against drops in self-esteem and feelings of rejection, which usually come with the end of a relationship. It is a form of electronic painkiller for heartbreak. It is like in the movie *When Harry Met Sally*, when the two heartbroken characters watch the same TV show in their separate apartments, while talking to each other on the phone.

A key question we need to ask ourselves at this point is: If we all have the same brains, which want to belong and are easily addicted, how come some of us avoid these addictions and build an Excellence Habit and a fulfilling life, and others don't? We can all agree that high achievers do many things well, especially when they are convinced that excellence is expected and required. By comparison, low achievers usually have a hard time getting motivated and end up eating the dust behind everyone else. This is a neat simplification that reflects our basic view of achievement. However, a study conducted by University of Florida researcher William Hart discovered a scenario that turns this picture upside down.

To evaluate how participants' attitudes toward achievement affect their actual performances, researchers conducted multiple studies. In one study, all participants were primed with high-achievement terms. Words like "winning," "excellence," and others were flashed on a screen. Each word appeared too quickly for conscious consideration. As expected, those with high-achievement motivation performed much better on tasks after being primed like that. Those with low-achievement motivation did not perform so well.

In another experiment, participants completing word-search puzzles were interrupted and then given the choice to continue or switch to a more pleasant task. Those with high-achievement motivation were more likely to return to the original task than the underachievers. No surprises again— both studies reinforced what we know about high and low achievers. The third one, however, offered a twister.

Like in the original experiment, all participants were primed with excellence words like "compete," "win," and "excel." Then, they were asked to complete a word-search puzzle. However, instead of describing the task as a serious test of verbal proficiency, the researchers called it fun. This one small change caused the participants with high-achievement motivation to do significantly worse than the underachievers.

For some reason "fun" undercut the desire of the overachievers to excel at the task at hand. How can something be both fun and a credible measure of achievement? On the other hand, the low achievers, primed with the same high-achievement words, perceived a fun task as worthwhile. Both their motivation and their ability to excel were improved. Yes—you read that right. In addition to their motivation, the underachievers' ability to excel was improved, when the task was described as fun. On the flip side, for the high achievers, defining or even describing tasks as enjoyable may actually undercut their performance. And when their task is introduced as serious or urgent, low-motivated individuals underperform. Simplistic as it may seem, if we wanted the best results from high achievers, we need to make sure they think of their assignments as serious and important. And when we want to get low achievers to outperform themselves, then it is best to structure their assignments around the concept of fun.

This is a small but critical insight. When building an Excellence Habit, a little self-knowledge can go a long way. When our rational brain is not natively wired to work with our personal motivational mold, then this mold can work against us. It becomes necessary to have a second look at how we motivate ourselves. When some of us have difficulties getting motivated at work, then it is time to examine more closely what kind of achiever we are. The motivational dynamics we rely on may not be the best fit.

Many of us get caught in the mainstream idea that assumes motivation is always available as long as we have enough desire and will. Not so, says research. Our brains are powerful pattern-detecting machines, structured to follow the path of least resistance, and often guided by a reward center that is easily hijacked. Therefore, to build excellence as a habit, we need to get to know ourselves. The good news is that we already know what we like and dislike. We have a history of achievement, or lack of one. We just need to identify and articulate what motivates us to excel and make it a habit to use this motivation. In a way, we need to trick ourselves into getting addicted to excellence.

THE N-EFFECT

The kind of motivation we respond to is an aspect of our self-discovery. Another such aspect is our level of competitiveness. Are we getting encouraged or discouraged if we are about to compete against a large number of contenders? Of if we are competing against one, do we prefer for all to see the results? Or are we going to do better if we shared the results just with our inner circle?

When the number of total competitors we are about to face reduces our motivation to compete, we have the N-Effect. Psychologists have identified this phenomenon by studying SAT and CRT scores. There is a significant inverse correlation between the test results and the number of test takers in a given location. Even when controlling for other variables, the more test takers in a given location, the worse the scores.

A similar study looked at the speed of the test takers. When told to complete their work faster, those competing against ten finished much faster than those competing against one hundred. Since this seems to be a universal effect, to improve performance we could use self-awareness. If we detect a situation where we feel affected by the size of our perceived competition, we could try to recognize that nothing other than how we feel has changed. Whether we see it or not, the competition for a test, or for college admissions, or for a job is still the same. The fact that we learned that we are competing against one hundred does not make us less competent, less prepared, or less experienced. Why should it make us less motivated?

Another factor that affects our motivation is performance feedback and, more precisely, when we expect to receive it. Keri Kettle and Gerald Haubl from the University of Alberta tested the theory that when feedback is anticipated sooner, it can positively affect scores. Participants in the research study took a test. Some of them were told that the teacher would provide grading and feedback on the following day, and others were told they would receive their grades in a week. Students who expected rapid feedback did significantly better. Across the full range of scores, the grades of those expecting next-day feedback were twenty-two-percentile ranks higher than the grades of those expecting feedback in a week. In other words, the way to motivate ourselves for excellent performance in any task is to imagine that we are getting immediate feedback.

FOUR

"MOVE YOUR OWN CHEESE" FOR ORGANIZATIONS

As a Ph.D. student at the University of South Carolina–Columbia, Taffy Williams had been working in the lab for six months, with no results to show for it. One day, in his frustration, he went to his mentor:

"The experiment you gave me is not working, so give me something else to do!"

His mentor looked up from his own work and fired back, "You are not doing it right. Go back and figure out how to make it work!"

Within two weeks of this conversation, Taffy had figured out what the problem had been and made the experiment work. The results became the foundation of his dissertation. He ended up with six publications out of this and became one of the most productive graduate students to come out of that university. It all happened because he was pushed to look back, question why something wasn't working, and figure out how to make it work.

Today, Taffy Williams is the CEO and President of Colonial Technology Development Company and the author of the best-selling book *Think Agile — How Smart Entrepreneurs Adapt in Order to Succeed*. His experience spans more than thirty-five years in business and development of medical technologies. He serves as a board member for multiple medical and IT companies, and former positions include president and CEO of Photogen Technologies Inc., IMCOR Pharmaceutical Co., president and founder of InKine Pharmaceutical Company, and president of Heat Biologics. Taffy Williams has raised more than $150 million for various companies, authored eight patents and several patent applications, and has authored fifty-three scientific publications. And it all started in this one moment, when his mentor pushed back. We might say a small change in his mindset resulted in lifelong excellence and success. Taffy Williams built a set of excellence habits that started in science and applied in his business life later on. But how can someone's personal excellence habits become contagious in the businesses they lead?

Before we answer this question, a quick step back. For excellence in business we have to mention the seminal work of Thomas Peters and Robert Waterman, *In Search of Excellence.* This number one national best seller shaped the views of a generation. *In Search of Excellence — The Lessons from America's Best-Run Companies* is still the best collection of insights, ideas, and principles, which business leaders try to follow and apply. Peters and Waterman employ unparalleled scientific vigor in searching for the common principles that turn good companies into great ones. Their book is as thought-provoking as it is fun to read.

The business world, however, has changed since *In Search of Excellence* was first published. Some of the distinct changes that seem to work across the board are the need for speed and innovation within established companies. Minimum viable product, lean and on-demand delivery, agile development, inbound marketing, user experience design — these are some of the new concepts in business today. As these processes evolve, we see a growing trend toward applying concepts from software development and the start-up world. Because these concepts are effective, many of the excellence habits from the entrepreneurial ventures are taking hold in large businesses as well. To survive and move their own cheese, large established businesses cultivate entrepreneurial habits.

DESIGN, BUILD, LAUNCH, SURVIVE!

When we shift our focus to the world of entrepreneurship, we see why we have a different set of organizational habits. Before becoming great, smaller companies and start-ups need to design, build, launch, and survive. And the survival stage is the toughest. It is when a new product or service takes hold in the mind of the market and crosses the chasm between early adopters and mainstream customers. At this stage, resources may turn out to be the enemy of imagination. A case in point was the Internet bubble. We had countless millions of dollars going to innumerable dot-coms. Within a short time, both the money and the start-ups disappeared. Indeed, how can a company make anything happen in the market when they have an abundance of resources and lack of imagination? The more logical organizational response would be intellectual laziness.

That's why to learn about excellence in the realm of entrepreneurship, we learn and follow the concepts of agile and this is where Taffy Williams is one of the domain experts. He wrote *Think Agile* not as an academic but as a practicing entrepreneur and businessman, who has gone through all the stages of a company's lifecycle. This is a different kind of insight, and this is why I reached out to Taffy for an interview.

Intrigued by the topic of excellence, Taffy agreed to share his experience. Since he is in North Carolina and I am near Boston, we set up a call. He sounds energetic, helpful, and friendly. We pick up the conversation fast.

"Figuring out how to make something work, when it is not — this is critical. And it is the same in science as in business," says Taffy. "I did turn-arounds for about fourteen years, and it often was about fixing issues that started before you got there. So, we looked at the possibility of closing one business and filing for bankruptcy. We looked at what it would take. And then at the eleventh hour, before having to shut down, a deal came through that saved the business."

With these stories Taffy echoes *In Search of Excellence.* Successful companies have a bias for action. There is a preference to do something, anything, rather than to analyze a hypothetical. Decisiveness is critical. At the same time, Taffy is quick to point out:

"Part of the game is being able to stay functional long enough to allow for your lucky break to come. I personally believe that luck is part of every success story. Talent is important, but if you are at the wrong time, at the wrong place, things won't happen."

The theme of survival pops up again and again during our conversation. One of the key lessons from Taffy's experience is looking for multiple approaches to solving a problem. If the problem was lack of money, you have to simultaneously (not in a linear fashion) talk to investors, partners, and banks. Essentially exploring all possible solutions to the problem. Even in a successful business, developing multiple shots on a goal can increase the odds of greater success.

The flip side of this argument is that sometimes failure happens. Whether it was our fault or not, and regardless of perseverance and grit, we all will at one time or another face failure. What Taffy emphasizes is that as entrepreneurs we should not fail for lack of trying. And when we do fail, we should accept it, take pride in what we learned, acknowledge our hard work, and celebrate the fact that we tried. Success will ultimately be what we make it. If our goal is to be happy, then we are successful when we are happy. If you have a goal to be a billionaire, you won't be successful till you become a billionaire. It's the same with companies; they can set a goal to have positive cash flow and grow organically, while keeping all employees happy. Or they can set out to dominate their industry and become global leaders. In each case, applying the principles of excellence and of thinking agile, as Taffy puts it, will increase chances of success. As he so well explains in his book, entrepreneurial agility is not a new toolbox of skills taught at business school; it is a state of mind and way of being and seeing the world.

It is a way to anticipate, preempt, and respond to surprises, adversities, ambiguity, and opportunities.

Ironically, while entrepreneurs are typically risk takers, they can also be indecisive in certain situations. As Taffy points out, when overwhelmed by data, or facing multiple options, they may be unable to pull the trigger. The bias for action is another habit that translates well from personal to organizational action. When we cultivate a flexible mindset to overcome indecision, it becomes a contagious example. And personal example in start-ups is critical because the teams are small and everyone is watching the founder. It is a natural tendency for teams to emulate their leaders, and in start-ups this tendency is amplified.

Moving forward is always better than doing nothing. Even if the choice doesn't produce the expected results, we learn a lesson and move on. At times bad choices will give us information and ideas about how to make much better choices the next time. How do we rebound from mistakes and failures? Says Taffy:

"If you don't have a healthy ego, you probably shouldn't be an entrepreneur. It is not a question of whether the company will stumble but when and how badly. This requires entrepreneurs to be confident and aggressive as business people."

Confident and assertive business attitude is a learned behavior that can and will translate into an organizational habit. Once we cultivate it as a personal mindset habit, we can then train our teams to do the same. But what is the source of confidence? How do we cultivate it if we don't naturally have this tendency? How do we beat our own fear of failing?

To get more insights into these questions, I reached out to Alan Knitowski, cofounder and CEO of Phunware, an Austin start-up since 2009, and leader of Mobile-as-a-Service (MaaS). The company is a back-to-back recipient of the *Forbes* award for the 100 most promising companies in America, and is also a three-time *Inc.* award-winner for the fastest-growing companies in the United States.

A little background on the founder: Alan Knitowski grew up in Arizona to economically disadvantaged parents. Until the age of nineteen, he was five feet two inches tall and weighed 110 pounds. So he got tired of being told what he couldn't do because of his circumstances or his size. He got his bachelor's degree in industrial engineering from the University of Miami on an ROTC scholarship, and his master's degree in industrial engineering from the Georgia Institute of Technology. He served as a ranger-qualified captain in the United States Army Corps of Engineers and spent a year in Korea before transitioning to the private sector with Northern Telecom, later Nortel Networks. This is when he got his master's in business administration at the University of California at Berkeley. That launched Alan's years in Silicon Valley, where, among other things, he cofounded Telverse Communications, a next-generation advanced services ASP focused on wholesale communications services for carriers, service providers, and value-added resellers, which was acquired in July 2003 by Level 3

Communications. Knitowski's executive resumé and accomplishments include a list of companies acquired by the likes of Cisco Systems and Internet Security Systems (now part of IBM).

We get on a call after Alan has completed a major deal, giving his latest company extensive access to the Asian markets. It is a big win, yet one can always hear a certain level of humility in his voice:

"There is no magic formula to start-up success. It is a lot of dedicated tenacity to beat your own fear of failing. The persistence and dedication to simply exist, move forward, and continue to fight is outrageously important to young companies. So, part of the importance of being able to reach a successful outcome is, as boring as it sounds, to simply survive. If you could be lucky, rather than good, I would always take that first. And if you can be both lucky and good, than it maximizes your chances."

Surviving as a start-up requires having enough money to cover your expenses long enough to allow you to reach your business vision. In most cases, this involves talking with venture capital, private equity, or other institutional investment funds. Venture capitalists are not trained to say yes very much. Rather, they are trained how and why to say no or pass 99 percent of the time. So, statistically, it is very challenging to find the right fit, at the right time, with the right group, with the right fund, with the right capital available, and with the right investment focus. Clearly, getting all these things to intersect is a major challenge. We can further overlay market conditions—whether it is the month of August, for instance, and everybody is away on vacation, and it becomes clear how tough it can be.

Phunware, in general, was very lucky. They raised $20 million in their first five years and did not have any institutional funds. It is pretty unusual for a company to raise this amount of money and have no institutional representation. Subsequently, on their institutional round, they raised an additional $30 million. After that, Phunware also raised $12.5 million in convertible bridge financing as a prelude to a pending $40 million to $50 million on a growth financing round, in what would likely become their last round as a private company. The point is, even when you can raise these amounts, it is never a clean, simple, or easy process. In Knitowski's own words:

"Raising money feels a lot like trying to cage cats with pagers and cellphones. People are scattered all around the world and you are trying to get them all, both domestically and abroad, to simultaneously line up and agree on terms and timing. So, in retrospect, we had the benefit of having had the first five years of our existence tied to angel investors without a lot of the typical institutional pressures. Five years of working with such investors allowed us to have more control, drive the process, and pursue our vision while we were preparing the larger, institutionally based opportunity."

But while investments help a company achieve its vision faster, they also come at a price:

"In the last couple of years, after our first institutional round, we have a lot more masters to serve. Some are very aligned with what we want to do and some might not always have their interests aligned with ours. So, in summary, we never really felt like we had a big enough balance sheet, or enough people, or enough resources to do everything that we always wanted to do."

"But, with that being said, what we always had was a real passion, hunger, and thirst for being unique and moving things forward toward our core vision. Ultimately, that was being able to be something that people didn't think was possible. We built a fully integrated, horizontal multi-screen cloud platform with a full suite of vertical application solutions. That allowed Fortune 5000 companies to manage all of their application portfolios across all of the disparate devices, platforms, and operating systems that now exist in the multi-screen space."

This is another important aspect of success as a start-up. Having the passion and the drive to stay true to your vision and not to sell out.

An ambitious business vision is tough to build, but also gives you unique competitive advantages in the marketplace. In Knitowski's own words:

"When we started Phunware, the consensus was that we were trying to boil the ocean. If we were trying to be all things to all people, then we would likely be nothing to anyone. Over time, however, what we actually discovered was that our big bets were not only mobile first, native first, and "fully integrated with a single log-in" first, but that these core tenets were incredibly accurate of what unfolded in the marketplace. These early bets became our largest source of differentiation — both then and now — as every other would-be competitor was only funded to be a point solution rather than a comprehensive one.

"We currently see a lot of benefits to this unique differentiation. The traditional institutional funding sources originally funded everyone thinking that what worked on the Internet would also win on mobile. However, this just hasn't happened, and in fact, it has been the opposite of what was expected. With all of this noise underlying the challenges across managing, engaging, and monetizing these applications globally at scale, the real key now is to find the frequency and signal in all of that noise."

PEOPLE MATTERS

Another core source of differentiation for Phunware is their approach to corporate and investor communications, which is how they work to keep their investors happy. From day one through nearly seven years in, the company continues to send out a Phunware "Phlash" Report on a monthly basis. Their philosophy with respect to both their employees and their investors is to be extremely open, candid, and transparent about everything happening within the business. They share the good and the great, and also the bad and the problems. When I asked Knitowski what the Phunware corporate culture was like, he had a quick response:

"To be outrageously and brutally open, candid, and transparent to all of our stakeholders globally."

While that sounds really simple, it is much easier said than done. As an entrepreneur, money raising may be your most important skill.

Without money, all the vision in the world is, ultimately, not going to build anything. What Knitowski says about communications is significant. Never take money from people and then forget to communicate openly and regularly. Leaders should do this monthly, even though most management teams do not.

Unfortunately, the reality is that most entrepreneurs work extremely hard to raise money and then start building their business without keeping those who gave them the money in the loop or up-to-date. This approach is fatal, according to Knitowski. Because when things get hard, then your investors are much more likely to keep helping you if you kept them in the loop continuously. When you communicate openly, candidly, and transparently, then everyone is on the same sheet of paper and everyone can be part of the potential solution when tough times surface.

If there is one Excellence Habit that business organizations can learn from Alan Knitowski, it is this one. When stakeholders have followed you closely for all of that time, then if you need more help your shareholders will already be up-to-speed and much more inclined to assist. Because they are so used to getting all this information and feeling like a part of the internal team, they are more involved and likely to write another check or open their rolodexes. The more information they get, the more they know about your business. Not only can they potentially know better what customers and partners to recommend, but they can also potentially introduce you to other individual and institutional investors. As always, the more people know, the better equipped they are to potentially activate their personal networks for the benefit of your company and their investment in it.

While this sounds very simple, for some reason nobody does it. Start-ups and young companies often find it hard to compel themselves to do the right thing, even when they know what the right thing is. Continues Knitowski:

"When month after month you communicate and you really are not asking for help, when you do actually ask for help, you'll be amazed at the people willing to fight with you, to get you through those challenges. You don't have to be Hercules and attempt to do everything yourself. Unfortunately, people severely underestimate the power of these relationships and networks. Here, at Phunware, we have had over one hundred investors in our cap table because of the broad and wide angel investor participation over the years since we started. These angels have become some of our strongest advocates, and have opened up their networks and relationships for mutual benefit. They talk regularly about Phunware and become evangelists across all they do—all because of the common courtesy and respect of communicating every thirty days."

Many Phunware investors have suggested that they usually get less information about other companies they invest in even when they are on the boards of directors. As Knitowski's experience shows, over time, this regular communication becomes an amazingly valuable core asset.

One aspect of regular communication is self-awareness. When you cultivate openness and clear communication to everyone, that forces you to be extremely open and honest with yourself. There will be no inner graffiti that can prevent you from seeing your venture clearly when you compel yourself to communicate clearly to all investors and employees. My conversation with Knitowski then moves on to the Law of Not Selling Out and the Iceberg Principle. In his experience:

"I meet a ton of people who want the pot of gold at the end of the rainbow, but I don't often meet a lot of people who want to go through what you have to go through to get there from here. The sacrifices, the commitments, and the challenges that go on—there is a lot going on under the water that is separate from the tip of the iceberg that you see above the water. For a lot of companies, start-ups are a lot like making sausage. You don't always want to see what goes in to making the sausage, but you always want it to taste good at the end. Start-ups are just a ton of work for a long period of time and they require a persistent, dedicated focus on the outcome at all times. Ultimately, it's not the activities, but the results that matter. You and your team have to be willing to fight, claw, scream, and kick to move things forward and you should always assume that anything that can potentially go wrong, will go wrong. It's the equivalent of Murphy's Law for start-ups and it's not about being pessimistic. Rather, it is about being an experienced optimist and preparing for whatever the market may throw at you.

"The harsh reality of being an entrepreneur is that it often feels pretty lonely. What people don't see behind the scenes is what typically motivates you to do whatever is needed to move things forward. You have to get out of bed every day ready to fight and continue that day after day, week after week, month after month, and year after year. You have to know what to do when you get curve balls. You need to be self-aware what mental framework influences you. And you need to execute violently."

Alan goes on to share three of his favorite motivational videos. One of them is the football coach speech (delivered by Al Pacino) from the movie *Any Given Sunday*. We talk more about the line of framework that allows you to find confidence to pull off things you are not supposed to be able to pull off. Two of the links are music videos with the lyrics, which are the type of motivation that works for Alan. You can find the links at the author section of our blog at http://vladzachary.com/.

People have a belief system about what it really is like to be an entrepreneur, and there is a very fine line between raging success and spectacular failure. But it is a lot sexier to think about how perfectly everything goes, and how it just works, than it is to figure out all these nightmares that happen. We see how close some amazing successes were to complete failure. We hear this everywhere. As a company, Tesla is now a success, but at one point it came to near collapse. So did GoDaddy — coming so close to complete failure before it exploded and became an amazing success story. Twitter was something else that was recaptured and pivoted before it became Twitter. One of the biggest companies today — Apple — has a similar history of almost failing at one point. And we only learn about the ones that make it. The majority of new companies fail. So if, as an entrepreneur, you find yourself in this situation, I just want to repeat Taffy Williams' advice — make sure it was not for lack of trying.

Another crucial aspect of excellence in business organizations is who the employees feel they are accountable to. Do they answer to their boss, or to the customer? Do they feel accountable to one another? This is an essential principle that works for start-ups and for more established businesses as well. One example is Upshot Commerce, one of the first enterprise grade e-commerce platforms and with more than twenty years in business — a real veteran in that industry. In a conversation with Neal Kaiser, CEO and founder of Upshot Commerce, he points out that his team is really flat. The focus is on engineering excellence and on genuinely caring about your customers, and this is, ultimately, who the team feels accountable to.

One last outrageously important point is that not just the founders create businesses and make things happen, but also the rest of the employees who work for them. And, therein, lies a paradox. On the one hand, you want to keep your employees happy, and on the other, you need them to give you their best. The entrepreneur and the leader may need to go through the seven circles of hell to ensure their company survives. But how much of that burden can be passed on to the shoulders of the employees without breaking their motivation? I think the answer can be found at the Great Place to Work Institute's annual list of the world's best workplaces. Since its launch in 1976, the data analytics company SAS has been ranked consistently as one of the top companies to work for. In a recent radio interview the SAS cofounder and CEO Jim Goodnight summarized his view of how you can do that and still remain at the top of your industry:

"When you treat people like they make a difference, they will make a difference."

FIVE

DRIVERS OF OUR BEHAVIOR AND RESISTANCE

We all have our motivations, which are at the root of why we do what we do. Our motivations, however, are not always on our side. It is ironic and absurd when we self-sabotage, yet we all do it. It happens even as we try to be fully rational and act in our own best interest. We have seen the enemy and it is us. So, how do we motivate ourselves to do the work? Let me tell you the story of my service in the Bulgarian Army. It was about several eons ago...

At the time, serving in the military was the last thing I wanted to do. The law was clear: two whole years right after high school and everyone had to do it. Despite the fact that it felt like wasting the best years of my life, there was no other way. Once in the army, most of us felt the same. We all had one goal: survive till discharge. Life was on hold till that day. We knew that when the day came, it would be the single most outrageously fantastic day. We even had a nickname for it: "Uvo." Once in the army, all we wanted was civilian life. It got especially sensitive in the second year. Everybody became paranoid and started playing super safe in order to avoid screwing up Uvo and getting extra months of service. The tension in the final months was palpable.

When the day came, I traveled to my original garrison a couple of towns away. With my civilian clothes, I marched through the gates one last time. It felt like the greatest party of my life was about to start. Inside the admin building, behind an opening in the wall, a clerk handed me the discharge paper. It was very anticlimactic. "Is that it?" I asked. "Yep," responded the clerk and shut down his counter. Alone in the semi-dark, empty hallway, I had reached my Uvo. Never again was I going to be inside that garrison, inside the dark hallway. No army uniform ever again.

At that moment a curious thing happened. My heart sank. Had I just lost something? Did the two best years of my life just end? "Nah," I told myself. "The best is ahead of me." Yet, I pondered these questions on the trip home. We had a saying in the army: "You get over the bad memories!" So I decided that it must be like in the movie *Apocalypse Now*, when Martin Sheen said:

"When I was here, I wanted to be there. When I was there, all I could think of was getting back to the jungle."

We all face similar dilemmas. And it happens more often than we think. When we are at work, we daydream about our last vacation, or the next one. When we go on vacation we make sure there is Wi-Fi so we can check our e-mails. We miss our children as soon as they get on the school bus in the morning, and then we are all too tired to play with them in the evening. Examples abound. With all the added distraction from social media, the ever-increasing reach of our circles, and the nonstop information avalanche, it is surprising that anything gets done at all. It is all too easy to get distracted from our goals, from that big, shiny Uvo that we want. One of the captains in the army used to warn us: "Civilian life is much more unforgiving than you think." None of us believed him. "You've been institutionalized, Captain!" we used to tell him. "You've forgotten what it means to be free!" He just grinned. We were there, in the army, and we wanted desperately to be anywhere but there.

The truth is — there is no here versus there. With time we realize that here is the only place we can be. And we can choose to be present here and now, or let our minds drift. Now, the yearning to be someplace better is perfectly normal. It is almost universal and it does have its positives, too. The desire to improve our lives is a major motivational force. But which of the many roads do we take? And how do we reconcile this choice with our vision for ourselves?

Deep down we keep a dream or two alive. One day, we will write the next great American novel. Or finish that painting in the attic and make it a masterpiece. Or start that business we are always thinking about. One day. Not today, though, right? Today is already scheduled, right? Today, we are busy.

What I am getting at is the concept of Resistance. In his book *The War of Art,* author Steven Pressfield identifies the main enemy to creative and entrepreneurial work. Pressfield calls this enemy Resistance and it is a sneaky opponent. It stands between the life we live and the unlived life within us. Resistance is what blocks our road to there from here. Resistance is what keeps us from achieving our dreams. Can we use this? Can we learn from our own "not doing what we ought to be doing?" Writes Pressfield:

"Like a magnetized needle floating on a surface of oil, Resistance will unfailingly point to true North, meaning that calling or action it most wants to stop us from doing. We can use this. We can use it as a compass. We can navigate by Resistance, letting it guide us to that calling or action we must follow before all others. "

Like Jia Jiang, who devised a plan to get rejected one hundred times in one hundred days in order to beat his fear of rejection. In the process, he got famous, got a book deal, and got published. We, too, can face our Resistance and then follow the clues. To do this, we need to become aware of the many manifestations of Resistance. We need to be brutally honest with ourselves and to leave our comfort zones. This means doing things we are not very good at. Or not good at, yet. And this means doing them now. There is no better time than now. We will never be ready. If we reach "ready," this means we are comfortable. The point of this is to move outside of our comfort zone and learn to be productive while there. Then do it again, and again, and again. Until we build it into a habit. That would be an Excellence Habit.

TROUBLE AND RESISTANCE

At an early age, we learn to avoid the feeling associated with trouble. Most of us grow to understand that to get in trouble is to seek attention in a cheap way. We know that trouble is a false form of fame. In his book *The War of Art,* author Steven Pressfield calls trouble a form of Resistance. Any act that draws attention to us in a pain-free or artificial manner is a form of Resistance. We are not necessarily aware of this. Most of the people who get in trouble will deny they were seeking attention.

Does this mean people who get in trouble have bad character? Are they weak? Not really. Trouble is like the shirt we wear. It is our choice to wear that particular shirt. We have a general idea of what we want to communicate by wearing that shirt. Sometimes we show the world who we wish we were, as opposed to who we really are. But that shirt is not us. In a good story, character is revealed through action. In life, what we do when it matters most (or when in good fortune) is a better indicator of who we are. Like the bad boy who steals a car, only to get caught because he wouldn't run over a stray dog. Those who get in trouble usually don't have bad character. They are still struggling with Resistance.

What does it mean when grown folks get in trouble? They are still searching for their authentic life. There may be a lot of stress or none. They could own millions or be penniless. Married with kids or alone. And they get in trouble. They are still looking for their cheese. Or they found the cheese and it is too big and scary. "How am I going to write a movie script? Sell it, and convince the studio to hire me in the leading role? Who am I? Sylvester Stallone?" He was a nobody, too, when he did all these things. So, instead of doing the work, we play around. We try to figure out if there is an easier way. This is how we open the door for trouble. A pro will banish from her world all sources of trouble — internal and external. Why? Because they prevent her from doing her real work, living her real, authentic life, and achieving her big goal. How do we break away from trouble, from bad habits if we want to become that pro? Where do we find this authentic life? I don't believe there is a secret formula. I believe in doing the right thing and letting the chips fall where they may.

Ray Bradbury, author of *Fahrenheit 451*, had a "Don't Think!" sticker above his typewriter. It helped him focus on doing his work. My sticker says "Don't Look!" We can't find what we are searching for with our eyes. Our eyes are for looking at the world around, at the Universe. What we want is inside of us. Sometimes, it is relatively easy to find and sometimes it is buried deep. Our authentic life emerges when we do what brings true joy, helps others, and is in true harmony with the world.

Resistance and Exile

In his seminal work *The Hero With A Thousand Faces,* mythologist Joseph Campbell argues that all stories we tell follow the same blueprint. From *Cinderella,* to *Mad Max,* to *The Bridges of Madison County,* or *Mission Impossible 8,* we have an infinite number of forms of the same journey. The main hero departs on an adventure. He or she is on a quest for meaning, justice, self-discovery, or revenge. After facing countless obstacles, she returns, changed or unchanged as the case may be. The return often is the most difficult part, and it usually makes or breaks the hero and the story. In most cases the hero was changed, but her original world is the same. The hero had her adventure, survived hearing the siren's call, kissed a girl with a dragon tattoo, saved the Earth from aliens, or had an affair. But the world doesn't know what this feels like. Often the world doesn't even notice. The hero might spend the rest of her days without anyone ever knowing what she lived through. This is exile. Deafening silence takes over after the thrill of the adventure. Everyday life is different after walking on the moon. The hero deals with the unsettling sensation of being back, but not really being home.

Allowing this feeling of exile in our lives is a form of resistance. Even the writer, who sits alone, typing away the day, even she is not alone. She is inside her work, with her characters. For her they are more vivid and interesting than the people in her real life. It has to be this way. In order for her to create a good book, which keeps the reader till the last page, she needs to imagine these characters more authentic than real life and hope to capture this authenticity on the empty page.

What about exile in our daily lives? We have all experienced it at one point or another. We have all had to return from a life less ordinary to the daily routine. Anytime we achieve a big goal, we can experience this feeling of disconnect from the world. We have changed, grown, but the world is the same. It is a feeling of dissonance, a lack of harmony between us and our familiar places and people. Do we miss the adversity, the fight? Or do we miss having the big goal? Perhaps a bit of both. I believe we owe it to ourselves and to our children to build a long and fulfilling life, and this means dealing with our resistance and feeling of exile.

Another barrier and a form of exile is fear of success. Even if we believe this is ridiculous and not applicable to us, it is still very real. Success often feels like drawing the attention to us in a large crowd. Everybody is minding their own business, and we need to raise our hand and interrupt them all: "Hey, look at me for a moment! I've got a great piece of work here!" There is a natural awkwardness that comes with an act like this. We resist raising our hand. Our work should speak for itself. Well, even Shakespeare had to raise his hand and promote his first works to get noticed. So, raise your hand. And while imagining a better future, let's also imagine a better self. Unless we give our power away, we are in charge of creating our future. Let's find our inner graffiti and wipe the walls clean. Let's fix the broken windows inside and create a mental context that matches the tasks ahead. When we start spending time on improving the small things inside, the big things in our way don't look that big anymore. We are not perfect and will never be. However, the reason to pursue excellence is not perfection. Excellence is about being the best we can be and living our best life.

THE "I COULD HAVE BEEN SOMEBODY" REGRET

As children, we find everything fascinating. These days, as my kids grow, I keep marveling at how energized they can get at even the most mundane trigger. Kids are like that. They could receive a hand-drawn paper heart and become super-excited. They could receive a Disney vacation and become just as super-excited as they were by the hand-drawn paper heart. As we grow into adulthood, we learn to match our excitement to the circumstances. Paper hearts become less important than vacations. Then, we reach a stage when we look for small things that can bring big excitement down the road. Like a hand-drawn paper heart for Valentine's Day that in a few years might become a Disney vacation with the same person and the kids that you now share.

As grown-ups, we do this more often. We plan for the future. We pick a programming major in college and dream someday to start a company like Bill Gates or Mark Zuckerberg. Or we choose journalism and hope to have a career like Walter Cronkite or Oprah. Or we join the football team and imagine one day we might be drafted into the NFL. The majority of us never make it to the NFL, or to the success and prominence of Cronkite, Gates, Oprah, or Zuckerberg. We accept this. It is part of being comfortable adults. We realize that it is not possible to reach and fulfill all dreams. Despite that, some find ways to be truly content and happy with their lives. Others, however, are left with this almost subconscious sense of lacking, a feeling that there was supposed to be something more. On rare moments of calm between jobs, spouses, kids, vacations, homes, career moves, cars, friends, pets, and in-laws, we remember those plans we had for our lives. Those old plans can often trigger nostalgia and sadness. We can find ourselves thinking, "I could have been somebody! Somebody better!"

If you ever get to a moment like that, I want to say to you, "Don't be that tiger!" Keep your chin up and maintain a positive attitude. It's not worth it to go to the dark side. However your life has evolved, it was for a reason, and we can only connect the dots looking back. If you feel as though you are at some sort of a midpoint and stuck in a position you are not happy with, do something about it. It still is a midpoint. Move your own cheese. Find the small changes that will make a big difference. Conquer your fears by doing the work. Be the warrior, the Spartan who keeps fighting even in the face of a million enemies. You will discover one day, I promise you, that the fight was worth it. The fight is what keeps us strong. And as you embark on changing your life midcourse, do it well. Build it with excellence and build excellence as a habit. Things will rarely feel perfect. But if you made it a habit to try your best, you did the right thing. And if you believe in what you are doing, then you can have comfort in knowing you stayed true to yourself. And you'll never have to think again "I could have been somebody!" You already are.

Don't be stuck in a storm. Be the storm.

Godspeed, good luck, and thank you.

INSTEAD OF APPENDIX

TOOLS AND SKILLS FOR EXCELLENCE IN YOUR CAREER

"I'm convinced that all great art is personal. So deeply personal that it magically transforms into the universal, and if you're Thucydides, or Copernicus, or Plath, your work transcends time.

While it isn't necessary to "know" the artist to appreciate the art, artists in training can learn indispensable lessons about the inner war and how to keep on keeping on by piecing together the life histories of those who seemingly pulled genius out of thin air."

~ Shawn Coyne

Building excellence in your career is more of an art form than a science. That is why I share the quote above. Instead of the traditional appendix, I have compiled a collection of tools and skills that have been helpful in my post-MBA career, and also helped the careers of others. What follows is by no means a complete list. If, as you go through these pages, you think of a great tool for self-discovery or an interesting study that has helped a great deal in your career, please, go to the contact section of http://vladzachary.com/ and share it with the Excellence Habit community. We would love to hear from you.

STARTING POINT – THE PERSONALITY TYPE

Although every individual is unique, people of the same personality type have a remarkable amount of traits in common. This is especially true when we look at the type of careers, in which different temperaments find satisfaction and success. Theories and models about personality types have long proposed to provide a way by which we can assess our characteristics and map others in relation to us. While we engage in this type of analysis, it is important to remember professor Nick Haslam from the University of Melbourne, Australia, who points out that personality is different from intelligence. According to professor Haslam, most psychologists consider personality to involve five main dimensions: extroversion-introversion, conscientiousness, agreeableness, neuroticism, and openness to experience.

Haslam is among the majority who favor the use of personality tests as a forecasting tool and a good predictor for corporate businesses looking to diversify their workforce. Here are some insights from his research:

- People who are more conscientious, tend to live longer.
- People who tend to be more agreeable than others, tend to be better business partners.
- People who are more neurotic, are more vulnerable to developing depression.

All of these personality characteristics are related to things that matter in everyday life. In a practical sense, while qualifications, training, and skills are part of hiring considerations, so, too, is personality. Some argue it is the most critical, as hiring managers often will subconsciously ignore a more qualified candidate, in favor of a less qualified one, who is more likable. This leads us to two very important questions:

What can we do to manage how we are perceived at work, at a job interview, in our social circles? Can we change aspects of our real personality to better fit our goals and desires without compromising our integrity or authenticity?

To answer both these questions we need to learn about ourselves in an objective, practical manner, and the personality type classifications provide one way to do this. Many psychologists admit that we have limited knowledge of ourselves. Most of us think we're above average in pretty much anything and if we were to benefit from a personality test, we really need some way of knowing that we are responding objectively.

In addition to objectivity, it is crucial to match the way we learn about ourselves, with the particular goals for this learning. Some people struggle with suppressed pain and childhood trauma, and their subconscious goal is to resolve this pain. Others are focused on improving relationship and family issues. There is also a vast majority of working-age professionals who have career-related or self-actualization problems. Regardless of the reason, for which one decides to pursue knowledge of the self, it is important to match the test with the goal. For instance, the Myers-Briggs Type Indicator is widely used for business purposes, and to help individuals choose the right career path.

Paul and Barbara Tieger, authors of *The Art of Speed-Reading People*, developed another excellent system focused on better communication. Their test and the Myers-Briggs are great starting points for self-knowledge. In any case, it is important to understand that the goal of knowing about personality type, is to understand and appreciate differences between people.

We should remember that all personality types are equal, and there is no best type. The different test and instruments will sort for preferences and will not measure trait, ability, or character.

THE SEVEN COMPONENTS OF PERCEPTION

As we work on learning about the self and improving how others perceive us, it would help to learn about what influences perception. The seven major elements that influence people's perception are cultural, personality, friends and family, regional background, gender, race and religion, and social skills. Learning about these components of perception can be beneficial for both our self-discovery journey and when we work on how others see us.

1. **Cultural Background.** Where we come from and how we were raised will have an impact on our behavior throughout life. Here are some examples of how the cultural background may affect perception at work: Someone from Eastern Europe might appear timid, passive, and uninterested. What team members might not know is that this person grew up in a society focused on collectivism. A key tenet in that person's value

system is the importance of being humble. Another example might be someone from Eastern Asia, where people appear agreeable, even when they disagree with what you are saying. They grew up in a society that believes it is impolite to say "no" directly, or create conflict in any way. Social harmony is a top value for someone like that.

2. **Personality.** We already covered why it is important to know your personality and to be able to speed-read others. Personality also affects how we perceive others and how we are being perceived. More introverted and analytical types, for instance, are generally perceived as less friendly, which often is inaccurate.

3. **Friends and Family.** This one is more obvious. We are close to our circle of relatives and friends, and their opinion matters to us. They will often play a significant role in how we perceive others. Further, for those who know our family, this knowledge will have an effect on their perception of us as well.

4. **Regional Background.** Do you consider yourself a Boston guy, or a New Yorker? A Southern California laid-back type, or do you identify more with the nerds from San Francisco and the Silicon Valley? Are you from Eastern India or from Mumbai? Mainland China, Beijing, or Hong Kong? We come from all corners of the world and eventually we build preferences and affinity toward certain places. The time we spent living in a region, especially during our formative years, will affect our identity. And we carry this identity wherever we go. Like Hollywood star Ben Affleck, who carries his passion for the Red Sox everywhere he goes. These preferences influence how we think and interact with others and, as a result, affect their perception of us.

5. **Gender.** This is another obvious one. We all automatically have opinions based on gender, it is inevitable. To change gender-related perception, or to eliminate its bias can be a daunting task. The fact that equal pay for women is still an issue is enough to illustrate this point.

6. **Race and Religion.** Unfortunately,

race and, to a great extent, religion, are still a major source of bias and influence on how people are perceived.

7. **Social Skills.** How comfortable are we expressing our genuine, authentic self in social or business situations? It starts with authenticity and goes on with your sense of tact and diplomacy, ability to listen, assertiveness, and ability to control your image, stand your ground, and be present, regardless of how a conversation evolves. All these traits and skills will have a major influence on how you are perceived.

BUILD YOUR BRAND, PROTECT YOUR NAME: WHY IS PERCEPTION MANAGEMENT IMPORTANT?

"Leadership is a performance. You have to be conscious about your behavior, because everyone else is."

~ *Carly Fiorina*

At the beginning of my Babson MBA adventure, a professor, describing the program, proclaimed that the graduate school had been directly linked to X number of marriages. "We don't keep track of the divorces," he added quickly. While funny, this remark was a memorable lesson. Don't keep track of the things that are not in your favor! In these first few weeks everyone who took the podium to talk to us focused on what a great school Babson was. We all agreed. We were all there because we believed the same thing. It seemed strange, however. It seemed they were trying to sell us something we had already bought into. As the workload steadily increased over the next few weeks, the stress took its toll. It felt good now, to be reminded that we were working toward a worthy goal, a higher purpose. We toiled in order to grow among a group of exceptional fellow students, and to learn from a leading, world-class academic team. We still believed we were part of a great school. Only after the workload went from intense to insane, did we start to feel differently. Looking back on that time, I now realize how important it was for all Babson teaching staff to keep building their brand. Telling us every day how lucky we were to be a part of this mad ride was essential. It played a crucial role both in our satisfaction with the program and our motivation and ability to go through it successfully.

The reinforcement of how good we are at our jobs is just as important for our success at work. As daily stress and workload occupy the minds of those around us, it is easy for our peers and supervisors to forget how valuable we are. So it is a good skill to learn to blow your own horn and keep telling the people around us about the great work we are doing. Sometimes it helps to remind ourselves, too.

THE POWER OF PERCEPTION AND PERSONALITY TYPES

Every day we are all being watched, judged, and perceived. In addition to our social and professional circles, we too, consciously or subconsciously, run a continuous evaluation of our behavior, our performance, our life. We also perceive and evaluate others, even close friends. "What do you think of Jamie? Did you notice she's a bit off today?" The impact of this perception happens quickly. Most times it takes a few seconds to form an opinion. Our brains are very good at it, because from an evolutionary perspective it may have been the difference between life and death. The ability to quickly tell friend from foe, benign from dangerous, honest from deceitful, relaxed from furious — these are all very basic paradigms that we choose almost automatically and often without noticing.

Even as we have little control over how others view us, we have control over our actions, which in turn can substantially affect how others perceive us. This obviously is not 100 percent proof, as the perception of others will often depend on their circumstances as well. Over time, however, we have a better chance to improve how we are perceived. To do this, we need reality checks.

We all have at some point in our lives encountered a sharp disconnect between how we think we are and how others see us. It can be a powerful wake-up call and a strong motivator for change. It can also be depressing, discouraging, and downright offensive. Regardless of how we feel, we still have the power to do something about it, in order to drive how we are perceived in the direction we want. It is our image and it is up to us to improve it. So, instead of waiting to hit this moment of truth, and have a shocking discovery about aspects of how others think of us, we can be proactive. There are many ways to do this.

THE FIVE STEPS TO EFFECTIVE PERCEPTION MANAGEMENT

"There is only one thing in life worse than being talked about, and this is not being talked about."

– Oscar Wilde

One morning in 1888 Alfred Nobel saw in the newspaper an obituary titled "The Merchant of Death is Dead". His brother had passed away and the newspaper mistakenly wrote about him, instead of his brother. As you can imagine, this must have been quite a shock. As the inventor of dynamite, Mr. Nobel didn't quite think this would be his legacy. Instead of being remembered as an inventor, a successful businessman, and a philanthropist, Mr. Nobel was the "Merchant of Death". Can you imagine a bigger wake-up call? It surely had a profound effect, because Alfred Nobel took his fortune and established the annual awards in his name. He chose to honor achievements in various fields that benefit mankind. After more than a century, the result is clear. Over time we have come to perceive Nobel as a name associated with the best minds on the planet.

Most of us have also experienced the occasional discrepancy between how we think we are perceived, and what others actually think of us. Sometimes we may think we are doing great on the job, and then we get an average performance review. Or we may believe we really screwed up, and then discover that everyone thought we did an outstanding job. Obviously some of these discrepancies are better than others. Ideally, we want to be aware, more or less, about what others think of us.

It is important to distinguish between awareness and feelings. Being aware is not the same as caring or feeling overly sensitive about what others think. We may be fully aware that our actions are not met with approval, and be totally comfortable with that. Sometimes important decisions that involve organizational and business change are met with disapproval at first. Awareness is about having the facts, and making adequate, rational decisions about yourself and your image. You want to build a successful career, and more often than not, you want to feel happy and excited about what you do. In order to do all that, having awareness about how others perceive you is very important. To learn about what others think of us, we need to ask them.

Before we go into the specifics of the steps to effective perception management, a warning of sorts. To discover how others look at us may be an overwhelming experience. Open conversations of this kind can bring unexpected revelations. Dismay, anxiety, or panic may crush you. This is why it is important to prepare yourself, mentally and emotionally, for possible surprises. Most people will spare us facts and details if they feel they might cause negative feelings. It is natural for the person giving the information to feel discomfort. This is why it is our job to set the tone right at the beginning of any dialogue like that. We will be most effective when we can have a relaxed, casual conversation. You want to avoid making it feel like an interrogation, or a business task.

It is best to be open and point out that your goal is self-awareness and self-improvement. Emphasize that you are asking for their help. It is also important for those giving you feedback to know and feel that you are grateful for honesty, even when negative information comes up.

1. **Identify how you think you are perceived.** Most of us have an idea of how others see us at work. However, we all know that we size each other up automatically when we see someone for the first time. It usually happens within seconds of meeting a new person, and often all follow-up interactions come only to confirm our initial perception. Think about all the times you met someone for the first time — a new boss, a coworker, a new neighbor, someone at school. We can often recall the first time we met. And once we form an opinion about the person, we then have the tendency to see facts that support our initial opinion. So the initial reaction transforms into a more stable perception. The same happens when others meet us. They form

an opinion about us, which then evolves into perception. What do you think these opinions are? How would you describe yourself, as seen by others? These questions are an important first step in proactive perception management. You need to articulate how, specifically, you think you are doing.

A good way to do this is to write down how you think others perceive you in areas that are critical for your career success. For instance, the job performance category would have your thoughts about how timely, diligent, and effective others think you are. Another category you might address is how easy it is to work with you. How responsive you are and how likely others will be to come to you for help is another possible area of interest. Choose categories to grade yourself, based on the performance review. Your company might have identified some metrics specific to the business you are in, which will be valuable for you to consider. So the first step is to write a profile of how you think you are seen, based on the metrics that are critical to your professional success and job satisfaction.

2. **Learn how you actually are perceived.** For this you need to set up honest conversations with people from your social or professional circles. It is crucial to make it easy for them to give you feedback. This will happen when there is trust, and trust usually comes with time. If someone just met you three months ago, they are probably not very likely to give you what you need. Constructive criticism is often hard to hear, and people have the tendency to avoid giving it. At this stage you are looking to get the most accurate picture possible of how people see you. This is why you need to ask even the tough questions about yourself and set up the conversation to achieve as much openness as possible.

Writing down your questions in advance will help you take the time to choose the right words and think through the kind of interactions you are about to engage in. Make sure you have enough time. Someone who is in a hurry and stressed about their next meeting might not have the right mindset to unlock the kind of feedback you need.

As you go into your sessions, remember that you are there to listen. Good listening and questions will coax more helpful information than any comment you might have. As hard as it may be, we need to stay away from getting defensive. Good listening is also about showing respect for the other person's opinion, which can further improve the information you get.

By the end of this stage you will likely have a pretty good idea of how you are perceived. Focus on those areas where there was agreement among the people giving you feedback. Are there surprises there? Did you expect something different? Whatever the case may be, you now have a good, realistic picture of how people perceive you. Time to go to the drawing board.

3. **Define how you want to be perceived.** As you go through these conversations from the previous stage, you will most likely start to

evolve how you want to be seen. We want to be successful and competent, and this process will help define more specifically how we want to be perceived. Details are important, and writing it down can help a lot. It is much easier to work off of a plan, which is on paper than off of one in our heads.

Key components of the blueprint should take into account the same categories you identified earlier in the self-evaluation stage. Hopefully you received some good feedback and can use these pointers for an initial draft. Then go bold. It's a plan, so experiment a little. Who do you want to be seen as? As in one of those popular social media quizzes, "Which Rock Star Are You?"

Does your plan involve career change or promotion? Even better. If you want to grow in the organization, write out how that would look. What kind of director do you want to be seen as? There is no harm if you act to build this perception before you actually get the promotion or initiate the career change.

4. **Take steps to change perception.** At this stage you need to take your plan from the previous step and make it actionable. What kind of change in your work and behavior can bring about the kind of perception change you planned? Your goal is to get noticed by those who matter most.

In both professional and social circles there are the so-called leaders of opinion. These people have the power to move how others think about issues or, in this case, how they think about a person. So, in line with your plan of how you want to be perceived, you want to make yourself visible, really stand out to the leaders of opinion.

Being visible is not just about being physically present. It's not about speaking up more often. You want to make yourself memorable. Distinguish yourself from the rest. What is it that you have that your more successful colleagues don't have?

Transform your work into your signature. Offer ideas, energy, and results that are unique, out of the box, memorable. As Seth Godin points out in his book *Purple Cow:*

"Something remarkable is worth talking about. Worth noticing. Exceptional. New. Interesting. It's a Purple Cow. Boring stuff is invisible."

5. **Build perception management into a habit.** Perception management would be most effective, when it becomes an ongoing activity. Up to the previous step, it is a onetime exercise. We can benefit from the results of this exercise even more when we make it a routine. Asking for feedback on a regular basis and taking steps to address any issues are powerful tools for career success. When you build yourself to be this kind of coworker, you have made a major step toward getting ahead and staying ahead.

LEVERAGING THE FOUR PRINCIPAL TEMPERAMENT TYPES

"You are not entitled to your opinion. You are entitled to your informed opinion. No one is entitled to be ignorant."

~ Harlan Ellison

Remember Mitt Romney? The usually even-keeled former CEO and presidential candidate? The "robot" as some would describe him. During a debate in Las Vegas when challenged by Rick Perry about once having employed illegal immigrants as lawn workers, Romney suddenly lost his cool. He initially answered with a chuckle, but when Perry kept interrupting, Romney's blood boiled. "Anderson?" he called the moderator, and, when no help arrived, he turned on Perry. His voice rose to a shout, his eyes flashing with anger. "Would you please wait? Are you just going to keep talking, or are you going to let me finish what I have to say?"

Moments later, Romney returned to his usual stiff movements and good cheer. Commentators swirled. What had just happened? How could Perry have so easily pierced the polished former CEC armor? Had we witnessed a flash of the "real Romney"? Had Perry been able to read and exploit a weakness in his opponent, or was it just sheer luck? The confrontation had hinted that perhaps there was more to Romney's temperamental makeup than the rehearsed, overly programmed manner usually ascribed to him.

The question that we often want to know the answer to is: What is the best way we can speed-read people when the stakes are high? To answer this, we need to dive deeper into the science and art of human nature.

When we talk about human nature in terms of temperament, we are talking about preferences. Temperament is how we choose to feel, think, and act. This choice will change over time and will vary with the circumstances. So if we label someone as an extrovert, for instance, this is only to describe that person's current set of preferences in regards to communication with others. So with this disclaimer, here are the four main temperament paradigms we talk about:

Extroversion and Introversion

Sensing and Intuition

Thinking and Feeling

Judging and Perceiving

There are sixteen combinations among these preferences and four distinct temperaments. Here are some of the benefits of learning to recognize these:

- Recognize the preferred communication styles of others.
- Identify the natural strengths and weaknesses of others and understand your own.
- Introduce your ideas in ways more likely to lead to the desired outcome.
- Recognize the four different temperaments, and cut to the chase with the right approach.

Wouldn't it be great if we had Superman's vision into other people's thinking? What are their likes and dislikes? What is the best way to approach them, to ignite in them an interest in our ideas or in what we are offering? In *The Art of Speed-Reading People,* Paul D. Tieger and Barbara Barron-Tieger show how easy it is to identify key personality characteristics and how to use this knowledge for more effective communication and faster results. Like many other works, their book draws on the same scientifically validated personality type models that most Fortune 500 companies use. Here is my interpretation of these four personality temperaments.

The Steady

Typically, this is the sensing-judging traditionalist. These people live in the moment and are responsible, straightforward, and consistent. Their core need in business and life is to be dependable, responsible, and able to execute well, without losing track of any details. The Steady respond best to precise, step-by-step instructions, detailed and immediate feedback, and compliments on their dependability and work ethic. They respond least well to anyone questioning their reliability, lack of understanding if they dropped the ball, and vague, open-ended questions or assignments. Obvious stress triggers for this type are significant change, midcourse departure from the original goals, and overall feeling of lack of control. They best cope with stress by deciding what actions to take, delegating, and prioritizing their to-do list. How can you help a Steady who is in distress? Take immediate, helpful action; use active listening to validate their concerns; assure them that you are on it!

We can recognize a Steady by the clues in their behavior and speech. Their demeanor is serious, responsible, and straightforward. The Steady will come across as consistent most of the time. They are polite, formal, well-mannered, and respectful. Although a core value is serving others, they usually have rather firm boundaries. They will stay within these boundaries, which in essence are defined based on their belief what the appropriate behavior is for various situations. The Steady don't stray frequently or easily from the way they believe things should be done.

The Driven

Typically The Driven are sensing-perceiving experiencers. They thrive on action and are easygoing, responsive, and informal. Their core need is to achieve significant, tangible results as quickly and efficiently as possible. The Driven strive for maximum autonomy and are most effective when they can establish a relaxed, down-to-earth, and even playful rapport with clients and coworkers. They respond best to fast, tangible results, instant rewards, and gratification. The Driven need explicit expectations, clear instructions, and short-term deadlines. They respond least well to formal bosses who take themselves too seriously. The Driven prefer a quick conversation to a long, written instruction or report. An authoritarian approach would make them feel overly controlled and would be another block to their performance.

The Driven are easy to recognize if one paid attention to their easygoing, seemingly carefree attitude. Often they can come across as happy-go-lucky. They are easy to be around because they like to have fun and have an inherently relaxed style. While not hurried, the Driven are typically always eager and ready to get into the next experience, whatever and whenever it might be. They live in the present moment and remain completely aware of what is going on.

The Analyst

Usually these are the intuitive-thinking type. They are conceptualizers who live in the future. Analysts are competent, logical, and objective. Their core need is to exceed their own very high standards. They want to be seen as strategic, big-idea, long-range thinkers. The Analyst responds best to expressed confidence in their ability to be top performers. They thrive on competition and reduced administrative responsibilities (leave those to the Steady, please). They love open-ended questions, which allow them to drive toward solutions. Their solutions. The Analyst responds least well to details, instructions, feedback, and examples. Any micromanagement, or even a hint that their competence is in question, can be huge obstacles. Other stress triggers for the Analyst are absence of logic, incompetence in others, inefficiency, and intense emotions, or drama. They prefer to focus on the big picture, consider the logical implications, prioritize, and then delegate the details. The Analyst is in their element when brainstorming new ideas, discussing future possibilities, and engaging in activities that allow them to shine.

Analysts are easy to spot as they are usually very confident in themselves and tend to inspire trust in others. They can occasionally become argumentative when challenged, and their characteristic overconfidence can make them seem dismissive or even arrogant. Often they love language, enjoy learning, and will demonstrate impressive, sophisticated vocabularies. Sometimes they have a tendency to overanalyze and are also good at playing devil's advocate. It is, in fact, a role they enjoy.

The Visionary

The typical Visionary are intuitive-feeling idealists. They think globally, strive to be original, and are value-driven and sensitive. Between building long-term relationships and reaching their ever-improving performance goals, the Visionary can be charismatic and inspired. They respond best to a highly supportive work environment and inspirational leadership. They thrive when they can have personal connections with their colleagues and receive sincere praise for their unique strengths and contributions. The Visionary is the type who doesn't do as well in transaction-rooted culture. They respond least well, when they are discouraged to bring their unique approach to their role and when constructive criticism is delivered too bluntly, without positive feedback first. Other stress triggers include conflict, criticism, and lack of personal connection. They can't stand going against their values or not being appreciated. To help a Visionary who is in distress—validate their feelings, complement their ideas, and express genuine sympathy.

The Visionary spend many of their waking hours thinking and talking about issues of global concern, especially ones that affect people. As a result, they often look as though they have a lot on their minds. Which they do. Since a central value for them is to understand people and the meaning of life, one can spot the Visionary by their communication. They ask more personal questions, reveal more about themselves, and usually have an intimate communication style.

#

These above described temperaments are just one possible set of shortcuts we use to simplify our understanding of human nature and to achieve better communication faster. Obviously, very few of us fall clearly within one single temperament type. We all have preferences that span two or more types, and depending on context, we might exhibit different traits and behaviors at different times. These temperament types are based on the generally accepted by psychologists paradigms that were mentioned before: extroversion vs. introversion, sensing vs. intuition, thinking vs. feeling, and judging vs. perceiving.

When we substitute these basic paradigms with others, like sources of motivation, for instance, or affinity/adversity to change, we can build a completely different picture of human nature. In some cases it is a fascinating picture. For instance, author Eileen O'Shea talks about the four temperaments as stabilizers, improvisers, catalysts, and theorists. She uses animal metaphors that have traditionally been associated with each temperament because this makes the theory more concrete and vivid.

Temperament theory is a way of understanding where our deepest source of motivation lies. The better we understand that, the more we can direct our life toward satisfying our needs, wants, and desires. It also allows us to understand others better and achieve fast, productive communication.

How to Survive and Thrive at Office Politics

Ignoring office politics is a sure way to get in trouble. If you think that the best way is to "tell it like it is," then you are setting yourself up. The complex dynamics of the relationships at the office are a "new normal," and we just need to accept this. So you have a choice, which comes down to two options: Engage and learn to survive, navigate, and even take advantage of office politics, or stay away from office politics and hope for the best. Clearly the second option is not recommended. Here are some habits, which once you get comfortable with, will pay off big dividends.

1. Learn who the leaders of opinion are, and keep track of their spheres of influence. In every organization there are decision makers, and surprisingly often, these are not the people in the corner office. Not on all subjects anyway. The formal leaders in the organization certainly are in a position to exert a lot of influence. However, they typically focus on the big-picture and strategic decisions. On the level of day-to-day operations and management, there are other, informal leaders, who usually are skilled at both their area of expertise and at office politics. Identifying and keeping track of who these influencers are is an important first step toward navigating office politics.

2. Have an agenda. This is good career advice, regardless of office politics. When you know what you are trying to achieve, you will be in a better position to articulate problems, solutions, and the reasons why the leaders of opinion would be better off supporting your worldview.

3. Create alliances. Who your friends are at work is not the same as who your friends are in general. If your success on the job requires you to have a relationship with someone you don't like, your best option still is to build this relationship and build it fast. You don't want to wait for anything to hit the fan and then to start looking for solutions without the support of the people you need. When you build these alliances, or friendships, at the workplace, you are not compromising your personal integrity. It is a sign of professionalism when you can keep your personal dislikes in check and focus on the common goals.

4. Seek to understand first. The key to a good relationship is in good listening skills and the ability to ask good questions. For this, you need to develop genuine interest in the people you work with and in their jobs, with all their problems, dilemmas, and triumphs. Once your coworker feels you understand where they are coming from and believes that you care, they will be more likely to listen back and support you. To do this well, you need to pay attention to what they are saying. You also need to pay attention to what you are doing while they are talking. Even if you are completely focused on what the other person is saying, they might doubt your attention, based on your nonverbal cues. The top three most important listening skills are unbreakable eye contact, nonverbal and verbal confirmation of what you are hearing, and appropriate reactions/responses.

5. Learn the trigger words and how to use them. Each workplace is a microsystem with its own culture, variations in language, and history. The trigger words in each office are the cultural hot buttons that get tempers boiling. And since office politics, more often than not, are about managing emotions, it is critical to know what triggers these emotions. The answer to this will define the political landscape. Knowing the trigger words has the power to redraw the org chart.

6. Take sides in line with your agenda. Many will advise you against taking sides, and this is correct when there is irrational conflict or emotions are out of control. However, on the business issues that concern you, it is better to have a clear opinion. The ability to articulate your stance and defend your position with rational arguments is practically a universal job requirement. Your position on issues will inevitably put you in one camp or another. When that happens, what you need to remember are your reasons for taking that side. And what you need to distance yourself from are the boiling emotions, which are so often associated with hot-button issues. One way to help defuse situations that are out of control is to look for win-win scenarios.

7. Stick to your Excellence Habits. Remember that how you achieve success is just as important as the success itself. The Iceberg Principle will remind you that most of your hard work will be underwater and invisible. The Law of Not Selling Out will help you stick to your principles. The Journey Mindset will allow you to keep everything in perspective. Other than that, always stay positive, avoid sending "Reply All" e-mails like the plague, and never start a drama on a Friday. Or any other day, really.

ACKNOWLEDGMENTS

This book was made possible because of the generous help and support of Alan Knitowski, Taffy Williams, Neal Kaiser, and Dr. Kerry Healey. They all agreed to be interviewed for the book. I also owe a ton of gratitude to my first readers, Dimitar Kotzev, Rob Olsson, and Michael Angelov, and my editor Ivan Kenneally. Thank you so much for your feedback and comments. I would also like to mention with gratitude Jason Stadtlander, Silvia Dubinski, Vikas Chawla, Michael Potts, Mason Fackert, Dave Rogenmoser, Polina. Thank you.

A special appreciation goes to Steven Pressfield, Shawn Coyne, and their relentless dedication to helping and inspiring authors in training. Without *The War of Art* and *The Story Grid,* and without the encouragement and insights from their blogs, I don't think my first book would have seen the light of day. Thank you.

Finally, the love, support, and patience of my family have been tremendous. Thank you.

www.ingramcontent.com/pod-product-compliance
Lightning Source LLC
Chambersburg PA
CBHW072133020426
42334CB00018B/1777